The 11
Immutable
Laws of Internet
Branding

The *11*
Immutable
Laws of Internet
Branding

Al Ries *and* Laura Ries

HarperBusiness
An Imprint of HarperCollins*Publishers*

HarperCollins books may be purchased for educational, business, or sales promotional use. For information please write: Special Markets Department, HarperCollins Publishers Inc., 10 East 53rd Street, New York, NY 10022.

FIRST EDITION

Printed on acid-free paper

Designed by Nancy B. Field

Library of Congress Cataloging-in-Publication Data
Ries, Al.
    The 11 immutable laws of Internet branding / Al Ries and Laura Ries.
      p. cm.
    Includes index.
    ISBN 0-06-019621-1
    1. Internet marketing. 2. Brand-name products—Management. I. Title:
Eleven immutable laws of internet branding. II. Ries, Laura. III. Title.
HF5415.1265.R53 2000
658.8'4—dc21   99-086018

00 01 02 03 04 ❖/RRD 10 9 8 7 6 5 4 3 2 1

Dedicated to the dotcoms
that are making our world
a better place to live

Contents

Contents

The **11**
Immutable
Laws of Internet
Branding

Introduction

Not long ago twenty-five-year-old Naval Ravikant had an idea: a Website devoted to "opinions" or reviews of anything a consumer could buy.

So far, he reasoned, the Web has a great number of online shopping guides that present quantitative data and comparisons of prices and product features but very little in the way of advice from people that consumers could trust.

Ravikant took his idea to twenty-seven-year-old Nirav Tolia, a manager of marketing at Yahoo! The two would-be entrepreneurs decided to start a new Internet company called Epinions.com.

It was a gutsy decision. Ravikant walked away from a job at Internet start-up At Home and $4 million in stock options. Tolia left $10 million in stock options at Yahoo!

In twelve weeks, the two Internet pioneers recruited four other partners and $8 million in venture capital, according to the *New York Times*. And recently Epinions raised $25 million in a second round of funding led by investment bank Goldman Sachs.

Will Epinions.com be a big success? Who knows? But the start-up does share four characteristics that are vital to any successful Internet brand.

Interactivity (Immutable Law #2)

The site will allow average consumers to register opinions about a wide variety of products and services. "Don't get mad, get even with Epinions.com." The most successful brands on the Internet will not be reprises of existing brands. They will be totally new brands with a focus on "interactivity."

On the other hand, a successful Internet brand doesn't necessarily have to be based on an original idea. Consumer reviews have been an essential part of the Amazon.com site for many years. What the Epinions.com founders did was to focus on this one aspect of Amazon.com and build an entire Website around it.

A Proper Name (Immutable Law #4)

Just because you have registered a word with the Trademark Division of the U.S. Commerce Department doesn't make it a real brand name.

There are two kinds of names: proper and common. A proper name is the name of a particular person, place, or thing. A common name is the name of a category that includes many people, places, or things.

Capitalizing a common name and marking it with an ® doesn't make the name a **proper** name in the mind of the prospect. Whether you read or hear a name, you convert that name into "sound" that the mind processes. Sounds cannot be capitalized.

"Epinions" is a real brand name, although the word is a contraction of two common words, *electronic opinions*. (The "dotcom" is a generic term that says Epinions is a brand name for an Internet Website.)

Would "Opinions.com" have worked as well? No. *Opinions* is a common word. There are many Websites with opinions. But only one Epinions. It's a real brand name.

Singularity (Immutable Law #5)

Epinions.com has already demonstrated one of the most important principles of Internet branding. To build a powerful brand, you need to be first in a new category. When you're first, you can preempt the category and block the competition. (Number two is nowhere on the Net.)

Furthermore, being first usually can generate an enormous amount of publicity. Epinions.com has already been the subject of a four-page article in the *New York Times Magazine*.

It would be ironic if Epinions.com had decided to launch the site with a big advertising campaign.

The world is awash in advertising that, after all, consists of the opinions of millions of manufacturers. At the opposite end of the spectrum are customers whose opinions seldom see the light of day. (Hey, Delta Airlines, when are you going to simplify your fare structures?)

Media are in the middle. They represent the opinion of third-party witnesses to the transactions. Their endorsements carry much more weight with consumers than advertising.

In the world of the Internet, you build brands with publicity. You maintain them with advertising.

Time (Immutable Law #8)

"Nothing," wrote Victor Hugo, "not even the armies of the night, can stop an idea whose time has come." The notion that an idea, no matter how revolutionary it might seem to be, can be uniquely attributed to a single individual is fallacious. A close look at history confirms that virtually all of the great revolutionary developments (the automobile, the airplane, the personal computer) were being explored simultaneously by many different entrepreneurs.

The ultimate winner is not always the person with the better idea. Often the winner is the person who acts first. To build a powerful Internet brand you need an idea, to be sure, but also a sense of urgency.

The Internet is the Wild West, the Gold Rush of '49, and the Oklahoma Land Grab all rolled up into one. Miss the Internet and you'll miss the opportunity of a lifetime.

In 1994, two grad students at Stanford University (Jerry Yang and David Filo) founded Yahoo!, an Internet search engine. Just five years later the company is worth $114 billion on the stock market.

The Internet is one of those "once-in-a-decade" revolutionary developments that will change many aspects of everyday life, some only remotely connected to the Web.

To put the Net in context, here is our selection of the most significant technological developments of each of the past five decades.

1950s	Television
1960s	Mainframe computer
1970s	Electronic chip
1980s	Personal computer
1990s	Internet

What's important to remember is that each of these developments contributed to a vast array of changes that ricocheted through almost every aspect of life.

Television in the fifties turned America into a stay-at-home society. TV changed radio from an entertainment to a music and news medium. TV changed politics from an issue-oriented competition to a personality-oriented one. TV changed our eating habits, how we get our news, and our preference in sports. (Baseball was the number one sport in America until TV arrived. Then football took over. The reason? Football provides better pictures for television.)

Television also affected world policy; it provided the pictures that drew us into wars like the ones in Bosnia, Kosovo, and Somalia. It showed us the travesties in Vietnam. And the successes of the Gulf War in Iraq.

What television did in the home in the fifties, the mainframe computer did in the workplace in the sixties. The computer revolutionized every aspect of business, not just in record keeping but also in manufacturing, distribution, and marketing.

Perhaps the mainframe computer's biggest impact had to do with the optimum size of a business. As a company gets bigger, it also becomes internally less efficient. Too many layers of management, too many channels of communications, too much time spent just keeping track of what others in the organization are doing.

The mainframe computer lifted the limits on the optimum size of a corporation. It literally made the superefficient, giant corporation possible and led directly to the globalization of business. (General Electric may have failed in the mainframe computer business, but the mainframe computer made GE the global corporation it is today.)

The electronic chip in the seventies was the "invisible" technological revolution. Today virtually every product, appliance, or device that uses power has a tiny electronic chip to control its operations. The automobile, the telephone, the camera, the VCR, the stove, the washer, the dryer, the electric toothbrush. It's hard to find a useful device that hasn't benefited from the electronic revolution.

"Pervasive" was the rallying cry of the electronics industry in the seventies. And it turned out to be true. The electronic chip had spread thoughout every industry in virtually every application possible. (It even got itself inserted into the human body as a pacemaker and in other "smart" devices. Your dog also can have a chip installed, making lost-dog flyers obsolete.)

The personal computer in the eighties cut across both the home and the office and revolutionized both. It put the typewriter and word-processing companies out of business and almost eliminated the secretarial profession.

Perhaps the most significant product introduction of the twentieth century was the August 1981 launch of the IBM PC. It directly led to the rise of Microsoft and Intel, two of the most powerful companies in the world. It spawned a huge industry that has since turned out a torrent of useful software products from spreadsheets to graphics to personal-finance software.

Some indication of the impact of the PC was *Time* magazine's selection of the personal computer as its "Man of the Year" for 1982.

The Internet in the nineties will take its place in history along with the personal computer, the electronic chip, the mainframe computer, and television. Five decades of incredible change that have revolutionized the way we live and work.

Of the five, the Internet will turn out to be the most important development, the one that will change your life in more ways than the other four.

And the changes have just begun. What's important to keep in mind is that the Internet will change your business even though you don't have a Website, you don't do business on the Internet, and your product or service will never be sold or advertised in cyberspace.

The Internet has changed the authors' lives, too. In the past year we have done extensive research on the Net, including material for this book. We have bought books, CDs, airline tickets, computers, furniture, artwork, office supplies, and even a dog on the Internet (poodles.com). Almost all of our recent strategy projects have been Internet-related.

One indication of the revolution ahead is the rapid growth of the World Wide Web itself. As of the turn of the century, there were more than nine million Websites on the Internet, 80 percent of which are dotcoms. And the number is growing at the rate of fifty thousand a week.

So fasten your seat belts and brace yourself for the ride of your life. This is the era of the Internet, and the future belongs to those who can do the best job of building their brands on the Net.

To that end, we dedicate this book.

1

The Law of Either/Or

*The Internet can be a business
or a medium, but not both.*

Putting your brand name on a Website doesn't make it an Internet brand. There are brands and there are Internet brands, and the two are quite different.

If you want to build an Internet brand, you shouldn't treat the Internet as a medium, you should treat it as a business.

But the Internet is a medium, you might be thinking, just like newspapers, magazines, radio, and television. Maybe so, but if you want to build a powerful Internet brand, you will have to treat the Internet as an opportunity, not as a medium. You will have to treat the Internet as a totally new business where the slate is wiped clean and where endless opportunities await those who can be first to create new categories in the mind.

- It wasn't ABC, NBC, CNN, the *New York Times,* the *Wall Street Journal, Time* magazine, *Business Week,* or *Newsweek* that created the most successful information site on the Internet. It was Yahoo!

9

- It wasn't Barnes & Noble, Waldenbooks, or Borders that created the most successful bookseller on the Internet. It was Amazon.com.

- It wasn't Sotheby's or Christie's that created the most successful auction site on the Internet. It was eBay.

- It wasn't AT&T, Microsoft, or Cablevision that built the most successful provider of Internet service. It was America Online.

Everyone knows the Internet will change their business as well as everybody else's business. But how? And what can you do about it? It's easy to err in one of two different ways. You can make either too much of the Internet or too little.

You make too much of the Net when you assume that it will completely replace traditional ways of doing business. No new medium has ever done that. Television didn't replace radio. Radio didn't replace magazines. And magazines didn't replace newspapers.

You make too little of the Net when you assume it will not affect your business at all. Every new medium has had some effect on every business, as it has had on existing media. Radio, for example, was primarily an entertainment medium until the arrival of television. Today radio is primarily a music, news, and talk medium.

Great, you might be thinking. We'll play the Internet right down the middle. Just treat it as another arrow in our marketing quiver. That would be your biggest mistake of all. You fracture your brand when you try to make it an Internet brand as well as a physical or real-world brand. No brand can be all things to all people. Yet that is what many Internet experts recommend.

To quote one Internet guru: "Internet commerce needs to be part of a broader electronic business strategy, a strategy that embraces all the ways that you let your customers do business with you electronically: by touch-tone phone, by fax, by e-mail, by kiosk, via handhelds, and via the Web."

Many brand owners follow this strategy. They carry their existing brands over to the Internet and wait for miracles to happen. So we have sites like the following:

- Levi.com, Dockers.com, Barbie.com

- ABC.com, Forbes.com, Washingtonpost.com

- Ford.com, GM.com, Daimlerchrysler.com

Does brand familiarity in the "outernet" foster interest in the Internet? A study by Forrester Research among sixteen- to twenty-two-year-olds says "no." According to the Cambridge, Massachusetts–based firm, "Some of the hottest brands in the off-line world have no online value."

That's not surprising. Did any nationally recognized newspaper or magazine make the transition to television? No, they were all failures on the tube, most notably *USA Today* and *Good Housekeeping*. (*USA Today on TV* lost an estimated $15 million the first year and was canceled during its second season.)

Business managers have much in common with military

generals who fight their next war with the previous war's weapons. Witness the wave of Websites that mimic the real world.

Slate magazine, introduced by Microsoft with a blaze of publicity, is a typical example. Edited by a semicelebrity (Michael Kinsley, made famous by CNN's *Crossfire*), *Slate* struggled along as a Web version of a conventional magazine, including a conventional subscription price of $29.95 a year.

Only twenty-eight thousand people subscribed. So *Slate* switched to a more typical Web subscription price, zero dollars a year. Traffic to the *Slate* site zoomed to nearly one million visitors a month. The question is, how will Microsoft make money by giving away the magazine?

The obvious answer is with advertising, which we don't think will work either (see Immutable Law #6). *Salon* magazine has been published on the Web ever since 1995. In spite of the fact that it has been attracting more than a million visitors a month, the publication is still unprofitable. Last year it posted revenues of just $3.5 million, mainly from advertising.

As a matter of fact, the magazine is not a good analogy for the Internet. Nor for that matter are radio, television, books, or newspapers. The Internet is the Internet, a unique new medium with its own unique new needs and requirements. Building a brand on the Internet cannot be done by using traditional brand-building strategies.

On the Internet, you should start the brand-building process by forgetting everything you have learned in the past and asking yourself these two questions:

1. What works on the Internet?

2. What doesn't work on the Internet?

Hopefully this book will provide the answers you need to build a powerful Internet brand. The material in this book is not based on strategies that have worked in other media. Rather, it is based on our experience with developing strategies for dozens of Internet start-ups. What worked and what didn't work.

Which leads to the first and most crucial decision you must make: For my product or service, is the Internet going to be a business or a medium?

If the Internet is going to be a business, then you must start from scratch. You must develop a totally new strategy, a totally new way of doing business, and (most important of all) a totally new name.

Who is going to win the Internet book war, Amazon.com, Barnesandnoble.com, or Borders.com? Is there any question in your mind that Amazon.com will be the big winner? There shouldn't be. If the Internet is a business, putting your name on both your physical store and your Website is a serious error.

Who is going to win the Internet bank war, Citibank.com, Chase.com, or BankofAmerica.com?

None of the above. The bank war will be won by one of the Internet-only bank start-ups, like WingspanBank.com. Why? Banking is going to be a business on the Internet, not a medium.

If the Internet is going to be a medium, then you can use

your existing brand name. The Internet becomes a complement to or replacement for existing media, be they radio, television, direct mail, newspapers, or magazines.

In truth, the Internet is a good information medium, an electronic library, if you will. Every company that has a sizable business needs a Website to keep its customers and prospects informed about the range of products and services it offers, as well as prices, delivery dates, warranties, colors, sizes, customer testimonials, and so on.

Instead of asking the customer to shuffle through out-of-date catalogs or spec sheets, a well-designed Website can present up-to-date information in a hierarchical and interactive way. (For the first time, a paperless office is within the realm of possibility.)

The Web should simplify many ordinary business transactions. If you want to subscribe to *Newsweek,* once you are connected to your service provider you should be able to type *www.newsweek.com* into your browser, go to the *Newsweek* site, and subscribe. Inputting your name, address, and credit card or bank account number should do it. No cards falling out of the magazine, no stamps, no trips to the post office, no phone calls.

In this example you'll notice that the product doesn't change. *Newsweek* is still a magazine delivered weekly by the U.S. Postal Service. The Internet is a medium that simplifies the selling of the product. It might also allow you to sample the product so you can decide whether or not you want to subscribe.

For some brands, of course, the Internet will replace existing distribution methods. (Any business that relies heavily on the telephone is a good candidate for moving to the Web. Flowers and pizza delivery are two obvious candidates.)

Three big brands that rely heavily on the phone (Dell, Cisco, and Charles Schwab) are moving to the Internet using their same names.

Dell Computer is in the process of shifting to selling on the Internet. It won't happen overnight, of course, but you can visualize the day when most of Dell's business will be done on the Net. (Currently the Internet accounts for 40 percent of the company's revenues.)

For Dell the Internet has paid off in more ways than just increased revenues. It has helped the company cut sales and administrative costs from 15 percent of revenues five years ago to an estimated 9 percent currently.

Cisco Systems, the world's largest supplier of network equipment, has also moved to the Net. Today Cisco conducts more than 75 percent of its business over the Internet. The move to the Internet has reduced the lead time needed to fill orders from three weeks to three days. While total revenue has grown 500 percent, the number of employees required to service requests has grown by only 1 percent.

Charles Schwab is also shifting from the phone to the Net. It has become the leading online broker with more than three million Internet accounts (and thousands more added daily). Today Schwab handles about 236,000 trades a day, 80 percent of which are placed electronically.

Initially, Charles Schwab thought it needed a separate name for its Internet operation, so it came up with the "eSchwab" name. Recently the company shortened the name to *www.Schwab.com*.

The Schwab situation illustrates two important principles. One, the same name can be used as long as your business will be moving to the Net. Two, on the Internet, the shorter the name the better. Charles Schwab is not a particularly long name, but the company decided to shorten it to "Schwab" on the Web.

If you have a choice, don't take a chance on a long name. When prospects have to type in a name on a keyboard, they are going to gravitate to the shorter names.

Merrill Lynch is also making a move to the Internet; presumably using both its existing name *(www.MerrillLynch.com)* and its initials *(ml.com)*. That is a mistake. Unlike Charles Schwab, Merrill Lynch is not going all the way. Its Internet move is only a half step. The firm obviously has no intention of giving up the 14,800 well-paid stockbrokers who generate most of its business.

The Merrill Lynch Website could function as an information source for the customers who do business with its brokers. But not as a separate business. If Merrill Lynch wants to use the Internet as a business, the firm needs to come up with a separate name (see Immutable Law #9).

With 30 to 35 percent of all stock trades by individuals already on the Internet, Merrill Lynch is in a different position than Schwab. It only has four choices:

1. Do nothing. Not a bad idea. There will always be people who want the personal attention of a financial consultant.

Furthermore, by doing nothing Merrill Lynch can portray the negative side of Internet trading. It's hard to badmouth the Charles Schwab competition when you are offering the same services as they are.

2. Make the same move that Charles Schwab did and shift the business to the Internet. It's probably too late in the game for this to work. Furthermore, what does the firm do with its fourteen thousand brokers and its reputation for service?

3. Set up an Internet brokerage business with a separate name. This is what Merrill Lynch should have done . . . years ago.

4. What they are doing, which is using the Merrill Lynch name on both businesses. This is a "foot-in-both-camps" strategy that will never work. In the long run it will seriously undermine the reputation of Merrill Lynch. It was just a year ago that Merrill's brokerage chief, John Steffens, publicly stated that "the do-it-yourself model of investing, centered on Internet trading, should be regarded as a serious threat to Americans' financial lives."

Trust is an important ingredient in any retail business. If your customers don't trust you, they are unlikely to continue to do business with you. You undermine that trust by speaking out of both sides of your mouth. A company should take a stand and stick with it. That's the way to build rapport with customers over a long period of time. Sometimes it's more important to be consistent than to be "right."

In any industry, there's room for multiple approaches, but there may not be room for multiple approaches in the same company under one brand. For many smaller companies, the best strategy might be to move lock, stock, and barrel to the Web.

Hoover's, Inc. started out as a bookstore and then a publisher of business books. Its first book, *Hoover's Handbook 1991: Profiles of Over 500 Major Corporations,* was an enormous success. The company went on to publish a number of other business and reference books.

Today, however, Hoover's, Inc. is primarily an Internet company selling corporate profiles and other reference material to a wide range of companies and institutions. Eighty-four percent of the company's revenues now come from its Web services.

Provident American was a small Hartford insurance company that decided to jump on the Net. So it sold off its traditional underwriting business and severed its relationships with some twenty thousand agents. Then it changed its name to HealthAxis.com and is now an Internet company selling health insurance from a variety of major carriers. Cutting out the middlemen, the company says, will allow it to market insurance at prices 15 percent lower than it had been selling offline.

Larry Latham was an auctioneer specializing in selling repossessed single-family homes in hotel ballrooms across the country. In spite of booming sales of $600 million a year, he decided to shut down his company's fourteen branch offices and move to the Internet. He hired a staff of twenty-two computer experts and renamed the company "Homebid.com." In a test of the site he sold 136 out of 147 homes over the Web at prices that averaged 97 percent of list.

Larger companies are big enough to have the resources to support both an Internet business and an offline business. In general, however, they need to differentiate between the two by giving their Internet business a different name.

Amway, the world's largest direct-sales company with $3 billion in annual sales, decided to take its unique distribution system to the Internet. But not with the Amway name. Its new Internet name is Quixtar.com.

Procter & Gamble is using the Web to sell beauty products, but not with Oil of Olay or any of its other brand names. Instead, P&G has created a new name (Reflect.com) and a new strategy. The site will allow consumers to "personalize" their selection of beauty products.

How can you tell whether the Internet is a business or a medium for your brand? You need to ask yourself the following questions:

1. **Is the brand tangible or intangible?** For tangible products the Internet tends to be a medium. For intangible products, a business. Intangible products that are particularly appropriate for Internet branding include banking, insurance, stock brokerage, and the like.

Online stock brokerages are just the tip of the Internet iceberg. We expect financial services of all types to move rapidly to the Net. The savings can be substantial. American Express estimates that it saves $1.00 every time a cardholder checks a balance on the Web rather than over the phone.

Travel is another category that is moving to the Web. In the past year the number of travelers using the Internet to book a trip has almost doubled, from 9 percent to 17 percent.

2. **Is the brand fashionable or not?** For fashionable products the Internet tends to be a medium. For other products, a business. Clothing is generally fashionable, while computers are generally not. Where fashion is the primary factor, it's difficult to imagine much business going to the Web.

We don't predict much success for Nordstromshoes.com, even though the site was launched with a $17 million advertising campaign. The commercials are amusing, but the prospect is unlikely to do much shoe buying on the Internet. There are three major questions a shoe site can't answer. Will they fit? Will they look good on my feet? Are they going to be comfortable?

3. **Is the product available in thousands of variations?** If so, the Internet tends to be a business. Books, for example. It's hard for an existing retail establishment to compete in a category with a bewildering array of choices. There's no way, for example, that a bookstore could stock all the titles available at Amazon.com.

Another category that seems likely to move to the Web is office supplies. Again, the choices are so overwhelming that no one physical store can carry everything a company might want to buy.

Product variation is likely to become a major battleground in an Internet-dominated economy. Excluding food stores, roughly half the people who shop at any given store today walk out without buying anything. The major reason: The store didn't have in stock the product the customer was looking for.

Now that customers have the ability to find anything they want on the Web, manufacturers need to respond in one of two ways.

If physical stores are your major distribution channel, then you need to reduce the product variety you offer. Compaq's best response to Dell, for example, would have been to reduce its product line and promote a handful of computer products available off the shelf in retail computer stores. When you make too many variations, you can be sure that the one model the prospect wants won't be in stock.

If the Internet is your major distribution channel, then you want to promote the wide range of models, sizes, and colors you have available.

4. Is low price a significant factor in the brand's purchase? If so, the Internet tends to be a business—eBay.com and Priceline.com, for example.

The ability of the buyer to quickly check prices on a large number of sites is making the Internet a very price-sensitive medium. There are even sites, like MySimon.com and DealTime.com, that will compare prices among other sites by sending out robots, or "bots," to check the prices. Heaven help you if you don't have a competitive price.

Because of this price pressure, one of the biggest challenges for building a brand on the Net is trying to figure out how to make money. This will be a critical issue for many brands.

Automobiles are another category where the Internet is likely to change buying patterns. Carpoint.msn.com, Autobytel.com and other car-buying sites are beginning to establish themselves as brands. The reason is simple: It's easy to make price comparisons on the Net. And there isn't any haggling with a salesperson.

5. Are shipping costs a significant factor as compared to the purchase price? If so, the Internet tends to be a medium. Groceries, for example. It's unlikely that Homegrocer.com, Webvan.com, Peapod.com, and other grocery sites on the Net will be able to build successful businesses and successful brands.

The milkman used to deliver fresh milk every morning. We're sure that many families would like their milk delivered today, but they can't get it. Why? It's not economical anymore.

The grocery clerk used to go in the back and get your selections off the shelves, but not anymore. Self-service is a lot more economical.

In the Internet era, are we going to go backward? Is self-service dead? We don't think so. Yet many marketing experts are saying the opposite. "The grocery store as we know it is going out of business," said former Procter & Gamble brand manager Doug Hall.

Futurist Faith Popcorn goes even further. By the year 2010, she predicts, 90 percent of all consumer products will be home-delivered. "They'll put a refrigerator in your garage and bar code your kitchen. Every week they'll restock your favorites, without your ever having to reorder. They'll even pick up your dry cleaning, return your videotapes, whatever you need."

The Internet is the biggest technological development of the twentieth century, but let's not get carried away. Just because something is possible doesn't make it likely to occur. The grocery business has three strikes against it: (1) high selection costs, that is, the costs involved in picking and packaging products in the warehouse; (2) high delivery costs; and (3) low margins. The average supermarket chain makes 1 or 2 percent net profit on sales.

It's hard to see how an Internet company could absorb the additional costs involved in picking, packaging, and delivery and still make money in a low-margin business. A niche market, to be sure, but not a mainstream brand.

Having said that, we can't claim to be on the side of the

angels. Last year the Webvan Group, an Internet grocery company, received the largest chunk of money doled out by venture capitalists, an astounding $275 million. In addition, Webvan managed to snag the former head of Andersen Consulting for its executive team. Somebody is going to wind up with egg on their face. Hopefully it won't be us.

Some consultants claim that you need both an Internet presence and a retail presence to be successful in the future, the so-called click and mortar strategy. Otherwise, goes the argument, how could you return items you ordered on the Net? That's one reason some experts have foolishly predicted that Barnesandnoble.com will eventually outsell Amazon.com.

Don't believe it. People don't buy things based on how easy they are to return. It's a factor, of course, but not the primary factor in deciding where to buy. Reputation, selection, and price are far more important. It's impossible to build a reputation as a store with great selection and low prices if you are schizophrenic, that is, if you have both physical stores and Internet sites. All you are doing is confusing people.

Will Sears.com become a big success? Unlikely.

No one factor, of course, will determine whether your brand should be a business on the Internet or whether the Net is just another medium to promote your brand. You have to carefully consider all the factors before you decide.

But decide you should before some other brand beats you to the punch.

The Law of Interactivity

*Without it, your Website and
your brand will go nowhere.*

Not since television took off in the early fifties has the
nation seen such a technological revolution as the
Internet. For a time, Internet usage was literally doubling
every month.

There is a relationship between television and the Internet.
Each is a communications medium. And nothing on earth
affects more people in a more powerful way than the introduction of a major new mass-communications medium.

Over the course of human history, there have been five
such introductions:

1. The book.

2. The newspaper, or periodical, which includes magazines.

3. Radio.

4. Television.

5. The Internet.

(While the telephone is a communication device and has had a long-lasting effect on people's lives, it does not possess the characteristics of a mass-communications medium.)

Life gets complicated. The new medium does not replace the old. Radio didn't replace newspapers or books. Television didn't replace radio. Rather, the new medium is layered on top of the old media, forever changing and modifying all of the existing media.

• The original mass-communications medium, of course, was the human voice, still an unusually effective way to send a message. Each major medium to follow became powerful in its own right because the medium possessed a unique and highly prized attribute.

• The book **multiplied** the number of people that could be reached by a single individual. Not only could millions of people share ideas and concepts, but these ideas could also easily flow from one generation to the next.

• The periodical added the attribute of **news.** Large numbers of people could share news of the latest events in their city or country and eventually the world. In essence, the periodical took the printing process used in book production and greatly sped it up. Where a book could take months to produce (and still does, unfortunately), a newspaper could be produced overnight.

• Radio added the attribute of the **human voice.** News and entertainment could be communicated with emotion and personality. A long line of celebrities have used the emotional power of radio to communicate in an exceptionally effective way—

26

Winston Churchill, Franklin D. Roosevelt, Rush Limbaugh, Dr. Laura Schlessinger, and Howard Stern, to name a few.

• Television added the attribute of **motion**. Radio, with moving pictures, if you will. Motion pictures, of course, were the precursor of television and still represent much of TV's content. Movies were, and still are, a powerful, emotional medium, but not a mass-communications medium. You have to go to a theater to see a film when it is first released.

• And the Internet? What attribute does the Internet bring to the communications table?

If the Internet is going to take its place alongside the other major media, it will be because it exploits a totally new attribute.

We believe that history will rank the Internet as the greatest of all media. And the reason is simple. The Internet is the only mass-communications medium that allows **interactivity**. (The leading Internet trade publication is called, appropriately enough, *Inter@ctive Week*.)

On the Internet a brand lives or dies in an interactive era. In the long run, interactivity will define what works on the Internet and what doesn't work. The secret to branding on the Internet is your ability to present your brand in such a way that your customers and prospects can *interact* with your message. You'll have to throw out many of the traditional ways of brand building.

Take advertising, for example. Will traditional advertising be effective on the Internet? Of course not.

27

Face the facts. People generally dislike advertising. Why do people love the TV remote control or zapper? It allows quick channel surfing when ads appear.

With the Internet, your prospects have total control of what they see, read, and hear. Is there any reason to doubt that they won't turn off your advertising message as soon as it starts?

Along with advertising, many of the traditional forms of communication are just not going to make it on the Net. Take newspapers and magazines as another example. Why would you assume that you could publish a successful magazine or newspaper on the Internet? Where is the interactivity?

About the only "interactivity" a newspaper or magazine format allows on the Net is the ability to read stories in any order you choose. But you can do that now with a paper publication. (Many newspaper readers start with the sports section. And *Playboy* "readers" have been known to start with the centerfold.)

Putting a print magazine on radio or television never worked either. Literally dozens of publications tried to take their successful print periodicals into the radio and television arena. They all failed. Why? The essence of radio is the human voice and the essence of television is motion. A printed piece just sits there; it says nothing and doesn't move.

Slate isn't the only Internet magazine that is slowly slipping out of sight. *Salon* magazine has been published on the Web for the past four years without creating much of an impact. In its last fiscal year *Salon*'s revenues were a minuscule $3.5 million, mostly from advertising.

TheStreet.com is a newspaper format trying to make it on

the Internet. In spite of a raft of publicity generated by its cofounder James Cramer, the site continues to generate nothing but red ink. With fewer than 100,000 subscribers and little advertising revenue, TheStreet.com will likely lose $36 million this year on revenues of just $30 million.

Advertising is drying up on the Internet as more and more companies recognize the futility of advertising in an interactive medium. Where do Internet sites spend most of their own advertising dollars? Surprisingly, it is not on the Net but in the traditional media of television, newspapers, and radio.

About the only successful publication on the Web is the Interactive Edition of the *Wall Street Journal,* which currently has more than 300,000 paying readers. With the booming stock market, a high-end publication directed at affluent readers makes a certain amount of sense.

One reason for its relative success, of course, is the price. The Interactive Edition of the *Journal* is a big bargain. While the regular paper subscription goes for $175 a year, the Interactive Edition is just $59 a year and is widely available for $39 a year.

We wonder whether or not Dow Jones would have been better off launching an Internet publication under a different name and with greater interactivity (see Immutable Law #9).

In this connection, look at the success of *60 Minutes,* a television show that was number one in the Nielsen ratings for a number of years. Although *60 Minutes* has a magazine-like look, it was created especially for television using a personality-driven format. Furthermore, *60 Minutes* did not lock itself into an existing magazine name.

What works in one medium won't necessarily work in another. As a matter of fact, chances are great that one medium's success will be another medium's failure.

- What newspaper also became a successful magazine brand? None that we know of. (The *Wall Street Journal* tried to introduce the *Wall Street Journal Magazine,* a publication that went nowhere.) The only successful newspaper "magazines" are the ones published on Sunday and given away free with the paper. Not exactly our idea of successful brands.

- What magazine also became a successful radio brand? None that we know of.

- What radio brand also became a successful television brand? None that we know of.

- What successful television brand also became a successful cable television brand? None that we know of.

The big cable television brands—HBO, ESPN, CNN, A&E, MTV, QVC, Showtime, and Nickelodeon—were not line extensions of broadcast brands. They were brands created especially for cable.

Yet too many companies lock themselves into the past. They look for ways to use yesterday's name on tomorrow's medium. News Corp., for example, the owner of *TV Guide* magazine, is using the *TV Guide* name on a cable channel as well as an Internet brand called TV Guide Online. Neither strategy is going to work.

If you want to build a brand on the Internet, you need to build a new brand designed specifically for the new medium. In other words, you have to build interactivity into your site, and you generally need a new name.

It bears repeating. The difference between the Internet and every other medium is interactivity. Unless your site has this crucial ingredient, it is going to get lost in cyberspace.

The competition is intense. There are already more dotcom Websites than there are registered trademarks filed in the United States.

Interactivity is not just the ability to select from a menu. (You can do that with a book or a magazine by looking at the index. You can also do that with a phone by pressing numbers. You can do that in a restaurant by asking for the wine list.)

Interactivity is the ability to type in your instructions and have the site deliver the information you requested in the form you requested it. Check out Amazon.com. Type in a subject and the site will present a list of books that match your category. You can do the same with authors or a title. (Instead of asking for the wine list, try asking the sommelier for a list of all French red wines that cost less than $40 a bottle. There's no interactivity in a restaurant menu and even less humor in a sommelier.)

Interactivity is also the ability of the site to furnish additional information based on your original query. Select a book to purchase at Amazon.com and the site will give you the names of at least three other books bought by previous buyers of the book you ordered.

Interactivity is also the ability to add your own information to the site. The best Internet sites are two-way streets. At Amazon.com you can rate books by giving them anywhere from one to five stars, and in addition you can submit short reviews, which are posted within hours under the book you reviewed.

Interactivity is also the ability of a site to handle complex pricing situations almost instantaneously. Take airline tickets, for example. An airline site is able to select from a multitude of fares, flights, dates, and conditions and give you a price on the spot, which you can either accept or decline. They can even recommend a flight schedule that offers the lowest priced fare. (The Cisco site is another Internet operation that makes good use of this on-the-spot pricing technology.)

Interactivity is also the ability of the site to perform a wide variety of tests: intelligence tests, driving tests, occupational aptitude tests, psychological tests. Some of these areas are going to turn into big brands and big businesses.

Interactivity is also the ability of the site to conduct auctions of all types. Priceline.com and eBay are two big brands that have already taken advantage of this capability. (Currently eBay is worth $18 billion on the stock market. And Priceline.com is worth $7.9 billion.)

Interactivity is also the ability of the site to diagnose a situation and suggest remedies. We worked with a famous personality to develop a personal Website. The first screen was going to be a menu of various problems that an individual might be experiencing.

"Don't do it that way," we suggested. "Make the screen inter-active. Ask the person a series of questions, then let your com-puter tell the individual what his or her problem might be."

Interactivity is a powerful metaphor for the patient-doctor or the student-teacher relationship.

You visit a medical doctor and describe your symptoms. The doctor diagnoses your problem and prescribes appropri-ate treatment. This is the kind of interactivity that is possible on the Internet.

Will the Internet spawn successful medical and educational brands? Why, of course. These are disciplines based on inter-activity.

Harcourt General is starting Harcourt University, an Inter-net high school for students who want to take high school equivalency exams. You can be sure that there will be hun-dreds of Harcourts to come.

Contrast correspondence courses by mail with Internet educational ventures. The best that current correspondence courses can accomplish is a weekly or semiweekly dose of interactivity. The Internet can greatly speed up the process.

3

The Law of the
Common Name

*The kiss of death for an Internet
brand is a common name.*

The most important marketing decision you can make is
what to name the product.

So we said in *Positioning: The Battle for Your Mind,* a book
published in 1980. So how does the Internet change the role
of the brand name?

In the positioning age, the name was important. In the
Internet age, the name is critical.

There's a reason for that. In pre-Internet days, a brand
always had a visual component. While the name was the most
important element, the visual also influenced the brand's purchase. The shape of a Coca-Cola bottle, the colors on a box of
Kodak film, the typography of an Intel logotype, the look and
location of a McDonald's restaurant.

The Internet wipes out the visual. To tap into a Website,
you type in a word. No pictures, no colors, no typography, no
look, no location.

If the name is critical, then why are most brand names on the Web so bad? That's putting it mildly. Most Internet brand names are not bad: They're terrible.

Some typical Internet brands include Advertising.com, Buy.com, Communities.com, Cooking.com, Cruise.com, Desktop.com, Flower.com, Garden.com, Gear.com, Gifts.com, Hardware.com, Hifi.com, HomePage.com, Images.com, Individual.com, Ingredients.com, Law.com, Mail.com, Office.com, Phone.com, Postcard.com, Sales.com, Songs.com, Sports.com, Tickets.com, Vote.com, Weather.com, Wine.com, Women.com.

None of these are small, insignificant companies. Major corporations or venture capitalists have heavily funded them all. Desktop.com, for example, just completed its first-round financing of $29 million. Phone.com has a market capitalization of $6.8 billion. Buy.com is planning to spend $50 million on advertising this year.

What's wrong with these brand names? They're all common, or generic, names.

A common noun is a word that designates any one of a class of beings or things. *Cars* is a common noun.

A proper noun is a word that designates a particular being or thing. *Mercedes-Benz* is a proper noun.

Traditionally, brand names have been proper nouns. (If you were a language purist or work for the U.S. Trademark Department, you would call brand names "proper adjectives," as in "Mercedes-Benz cars." But most people use brand names as nouns. They will say, "I drive a Mercedes," not "I drive a Mercedes car.")

The best-known, most valuable brand names in the world are all proper nouns, not common or generic names. There are sixty worldwide brands worth more than $1 billion each, according to Interbrand, a brand consulting group. And none of these are common or generic names.

Typical brands on the top sixty list include Coca-Cola, Microsoft, Ford, Disney, Intel, McDonald's, Marlboro, Nokia, Nescafé, Hewlett-Packard, Gillette, Kodak, and Sony. (Together, the sixty brands, according to Interbrand, are worth an incredible $729.4 billion.)

A few years from now are you likely to find Cola.com, Software.com, Cars.com, Kids.com, Chips.com, Hamburgers.com, Cigarettes.com, Cellphones.com, Coffee.com, Computers.com, Razors.com, Photos.com, or Electronics.com on the list of the world's most valuable names? We think not.

"But the Internet is different" is the cry you hear from thirty-year-old CEOs managing Internet start-ups. You don't have to wear suits, you don't have to wear ties, you don't have to wear shoes, you don't have to make money, you get stock options worth millions, and you can use generic names for your Websites.

But is it? Is the Internet really different when it comes to brand names? So far it doesn't seem to be.

- The leading Internet service provider is not ISP.com. It's AOL.

- The leading search engine on the Net is not Searchengine.com. It's Yahoo!

- The leading retailer of books on the Net is not Books.com. It's Amazon.com.

- The leading job-search site on the Net is not Jobs.com. It's Monster.com.

- The leading auction site on the Net is not Auction.com. It's eBay.

- The leading airline-ticket bid site on the Net is not Airlineticketbid.com. It's Priceline.com.

- The leading travel site on the Net is not Travel.com. It's Expedia.com.

- The leading electronic greeting card is not GreetingCard.com. It's Bluemountain.com.

As it happens, there are two Internet names on Interbrand's list of the sixty most valuable brands. AOL, worth $4.3 billion, and Yahoo!, worth $1.8 billion. You'll notice that both AOL and Yahoo! are proper nouns, not common nouns.

In spite of all the evidence to the contrary, why do most Internet executives continue to prefer using common names rather than proper names for their Websites? There are three reasons.

1. When the Internet was new, when there were few sites up and running, when few people knew the names of any Websites, a common name was an advantage. You wanted to look for a site selling shoes, you typed in "shoes.com."

   It was like an old-fashioned grocery store. You wanted

crackers, you asked for the crackers. You wanted oatmeal cookies, you asked for the oatmeal cookies. Today, however, there are many brands of cookies and many brands of crackers in a supermarket. You don't ask for crackers, you ask for Ritz crackers. You don't ask for oatmeal cookies, you ask for Pepperidge Farm oatmeal cookies.

2. When the Internet was new, many companies jumped on the Internet with common names. After all, a common name was the fastest, most direct way to communicate what the site was all about. The common name also made it easier for users to navigate the Net.

   The advantages of a common name lasted for about two weeks as thousands and then hundreds of thousands of Internet sites were set up. Today, with more than five million dotcoms in operation, the advantages of a common name for an Internet site are nil.

3. Now that the Net has been around for a few years, Internet companies are having trouble getting beyond the mind-set of those early days. They still think a common name is the best approach. In some ways, this is a self-reinforcing situation. As everyone launches common name sites, every newcomer thinks this must be the way to go. And so that's the way they go.

   With his *Candid Camera,* Allen Funt exploited human nature to do what others are doing regardless of whether or not it makes sense. His favorite episode involves an elevator where the first person goes into the car and faces the front. The next three people, all *Candid Camera* confederates, get into the elevator and face the rear. By the time the fourth person comes in, the first one feels so uncomfortable that he turns around and also faces the rear.

Face the facts. Just because most sites use common names doesn't mean that a common name is the best strategy for your site. It only means that most Internet operators are under group pressure to conform.

The Internet is so young that we haven't had the fallout that for sure is coming. Some samples of this common-noun craziness are as follows:

- In automobiles, we have AutoConnect.com, Autosite.com, AutoTrader.com, Autoweb.com, Cars.com, CarsDirect.com, and CarOrder.com.

- In banking, we have Ebank.com, Telebank.com, and Netbank.com.

- In diamonds, we have eDiamonds.com, InternetDiamonds.com, and WorldDiamonds.com.

- In employment, we have ComputerJobs.com, Gotajob.com, Headhunter.net, and Jobs.com.

- In facsimile, we have eFax.com, Fax.com, and Jfax.com.

- In finance, we have 401k.com, eCoverage.com, eCredit.com, Loansdirect.com, eHealthinsurance.com, eLoan.com, Loanwise.com, Mortgage.com, and Studentloan.com.

- In furniture, we have BeHome.com, Decoratewithstyle.com, Ezshop.com, Furniture.com, FurnitureFind.com, Furnitureonline.com, Housenet.com, and Living.com.

- In groceries, we have Food.com, NetGrocer.com, and HomeGrocer.com.

- In health and nutrition, we have eDiets.com, eNutrition.com, HealthQuick.com, and onHealth.com.

- In pets, we have Petco.com, Pets.com, and Petstore.com.

- In postage, we have E-Stamp.com, Stamps.com, and Simplepostage.com.

- In prescription drugs, we have Drugstore.com, YourPharmacy.com, and Rx.com.

- In real estate, we have Cyberhomes.com, eProperty.com, Goodhome.com, Homeadvisor.com, Homebid.com, Homegain.com, Homes.com, Homeseekers.com, Homestore.com, Myhome.com, Ourhouse.com, Owners.com, RealEstate.com, and Realtor.com.

- In shopping, we have IStopShop.com, Buy.com, BuyItNow.com, Netmarket.com, NowOnSpecial.com, ShopNow.com, and Shopping.com.

- In travel, we have Cheaptickets.com, Lowestfare.com, TravelHoliday.com, and Trip.com.

These are not generic names picked at random from the millions of dotcoms on the Internet. These are serious sites backed by serious venture capitalists and supported by millions of dollars' worth of advertising.

- Art.com is spending $18 million this year on advertising.

- AutoConnect.com is spending $15 million this year on advertising.

- CarsDirect is spending $30 million this year on advertising.

- Drugstore.com is spending $30 million this year on advertising.

- Homestore.com is spending $20 million this year on advertising.

- Living.com is spending $20 million this year on advertising.

- Pets.com is spending $20 million this year on advertising.

- Petstore.com is spending $10 million this year on advertising.

- RealEstate.com is spending $13 million this year on advertising.

- Rx.com is spending $13 million this year on advertising.

These CommonNameDot.coms are just a small sample of the thousands of Internet companies trying to spend their way into the prospect's mind. For the most part it is money down the rat hole. There's no way that even a small percentage of these common-name sites are going to make it.

(It's a sign of the times that one of the most heavily hyped advertising agencies specializing in the Internet field calls itself Agency.com.)

Will some of these generic names be successful? Sure. In the land of the blind, the one-eyed man is king. Nobody is going to stop drinking beer because all of the beer brands use generic names. Nobody is going to stop buying on the Web just because all the Internet brands are generic.

In the absence of competition, people will buy from a site with a common name. But as sites are set up with strong "proper" brand names, the common-name sites are going to dry up and blow away.

You have to win in the mind. And the mind treats common or generic names as representative of all the sites in the category. Not just a single site.

In the human mind all automotive sites are "car dotcoms." How can Cars.com ever establish a singular identity separate from the other car dotcoms?

In the mind all furniture sites are "furniture dotcoms." How can Furniture.com ever establish a singular identity separate from the rest of the furniture dotcoms?

The vast majority of brand names on the Web are purely generic names. Most of these sites are not going to go anywhere.

What's an eToys? An e-toy is a toy purchased on the Internet. An eToys is a company that sells e-toys on the Internet.

The name eToys is a weak brand name, yet the stock market thinks differently. On the first day that eToys went public, the stock price nearly quadrupled in value, making the company worth $7.7 billion, 35 percent greater than that of its retail rival, Toys "R" Us Inc. (In its last fiscal year eToys lost $73 million on revenues of $34.7 million.)

One of the problems with a common name like eToys is the ability of competition to jump in the marketplace and claim similar names.

- eToy.com

- iToy.com

- iToys.com

- Toy.com

- Toys.com

- Toystore.com

- iToystore.com

- eToystore.com

Naturally eToys will try to register these and other similar names (as they have already started to do). But where do you stop? How much will it cost you? And will the legal system allow one company to own all the sites with "toy" in the name?

What's an E*Trade? An e-trade is a stock purchase or sale made on the Internet. An E*Trade is a company that handles e-trades on the Internet.

A generic name like E*Trade is weak. The mind thinks verbally, not visually. E-trade is the name of the category, not the company. Furthermore, you can't use an asterisk in the actual site name. In order to reach E*Trade, you have to type in www.etrade.com.

Even though E*Trade has the enormous advantage of being first on the Internet, the company has already fallen to second place in terms of customer-trading volume online. (Charles Schwab is the leader.)

Massive advertising in the mass media is keeping E*Trade

in the game. But how long they will be able to keep up the advertising pressure in the face of enormous operating losses remains to be seen. (E*Trade lost $54 million on revenues of $662 million in its last fiscal year, yet the company has a market capitalization of $6.8 billion.)

How can we be so sure that proper names will prevail over common names as brand names on the Internet? The only proof we can offer you is a hundred years of history. In the past century, how many common names have become successful brands?

Very, very few.

Few categories in the outernet, as opposed to the Internet, are dominated by generic brand names. Invariably they are dominated by proper or "name" names.

- In automobiles, we have Ford, Chevrolet, Chrysler, Volvo, and Mercedes-Benz.

- In banking, we have Citibank, Chase Manhattan, and Wells Fargo.

- In drugstores, we have CVS, Eckerd, Rite-Aid, Walgreen's, and Osco.

- In furniture, we have Ikea, Ethan Allen, Levitz, Roche-Bobois, and Maurice Villency.

- In groceries, we have Kroger, Safeway, Winn-Dixie, Publix, and Pathmark.

- In department stores we have Macy's, Saks Fifth Avenue, Marshall Field, Nordstrom, and Neiman-Marcus.

- In discount stores we have Wal-Mart, Kmart, and Target.

45

But the Internet is different, you might be thinking. There must be a reason for the rash of generic names.

The Internet is different, but the mind of the prospect stays the same. To be successful you have to position your brand name in the mind.

What managers often forget is that the mind treats a generic or common word as the name for a category of things, not as one particular thing or brand.

No automobile dealer would call his or her dealership "Cars." Why not? Imagine the following conversation.

"Where did you buy your new car?"

"At Cars®."

"Huh. What did you say? I asked you what dealership you bought your new car from."

With literally thousands of Websites using generic names, you can expect the same type of dialog to occur.

"What discount broker do you use on the Internet?"

"Mydiscountbroker."

"I know, but what's his name?"

"Mydiscountbroker."

"I already asked you that."

This is not a laughing matter. It demonstrates the way the mind works. Words get put into categories. A common name gets put into a different category than a proper name.

The comedy team of Abbott and Costello based their classic baseball routine on the confusion that can occur when one class of words is substituted for another.

"Let's see, we have on the bags, Who's on first. What's on second. I Don't Know is on third."

"That's what I want to find out. Who's on first?

"Yes."

"I mean, the fellow's name?"

"Who."

"The first baseman?"

"Who."

"The guy playing first?"

"Who is on first."

"I'm asking *you*, who's on first?"

"That's the man's name."

"That's who's name?"

"Yes."

Many companies in the past hundred years have tried to use common-type nouns as brand names in their categories. Just check the trademark register. There's a host of brand names that have tried to preempt a category by using a common-sounding name. Some examples:

- Toast'em toaster pastries.

- Soft & Dri deodorant.

- Soft 'N Gentle toilet tissue.

- Soft Shave shaving cream.

- Nice 'N Soft facial tissues.

- NA nonalcoholic beer.

- Baby's Choice disposable diapers.

- Kid Care adhesive bandages.

47

Tell the truth. Do any of these generic brand names ring a bell with you? Probably not. It's hard to remember a brand that uses a common name.

One of the best examples of the futility of trying to build a brand with a common name is Lite, the first light beer. When Miller Brewing introduced Lite beer, there was no "Miller" on the can. And no competitor could use the word "Lite" on a beer brand either because Miller owned the trademark.

Miller launched Lite with a massive advertising program and the segment took off. As you might have expected, many competitors jumped in with generic versions of their own. Schlitz Light, Coors Light, Bud Light.

Even though Miller was first with Lite beer, even though Lite had the benefit of tremendous amounts of advertising and publicity, Miller was forced to throw in the towel and rename the product, Miller Lite.

You can see the problem. The beer drinker goes into the bar and says, "Give me a Lite beer." And the bartender says, "Fine. What kind of light beer do you want?"

Some categories, of course, are loaded with mostly generic brand names. (Group pressure at work.) What is interesting is that in these categories, generally no one brand will dominate the category. Breakfast cereals are a good example—brands like Corn Flakes, Bran Flakes, Frosted Flakes, and 100% Granola.

Take the "bran" category. There are dozens of "bran" brands trying to capture the category. Some examples:

- Kellogg's All-Bran

- Kellogg's Bran Flakes

- Kellogg's 40+ Bran Flakes

- Kellogg's Raisin Bran

- Nabisco 100% Bran

- Post Bran Flakes

- Post Raisin Bran

- Total Raisin Bran

As a result of the overwhelming reliance on common names, the cereal category has no clear-cut brand leader. The largest-selling cereal brand has a market share of about 6 percent. (Cheerios is one of the few cereal brands that doesn't use a common name.)

If common names don't work on the outernet, why should they work on the Internet? The problem is exactly the same. How do I get the prospect to remember my brand name and associate it with some positive attribute?

When you use a common name as a brand name, you have little chance to do either. First, the prospect can't differentiate between your site name and the category name. Second, you can't associate a specific attribute with the name because the name stands for the entire category, not just your site.

Some sites try to solve this problem by combining the attribute with the common noun. Instead of Books.com, the brand name becomes AllBooks4Less.com. Or perhaps Cheaptickets.com or Lowestfare.com.

Ironically, this is a branding strategy that can have a modicum of success in the outernet but not on the Internet. If you're driving down the road and see a sign that says "All Books 4 Less," you know what the store is selling and why you might want to shop there. (A chain named "All Books 4 Less," on the other hand, is still not going to outsell Barnes & Noble, Waldenbooks, or Borders.)

On the Internet you don't drive down the road and you don't see the AllBooks4Less sign. You are going to have to remember the name and that's not going to be easy.

You ask your mind, "Who sells all books for less on the Net?" And the answer comes back "Amazon.com."

In the short term, however, many prospects are going to use search engines to find sites that might interest them. So a name like AllBooks4Less.com could conceivably attract a fair number of hits. But that's only in the short term.

The whole idea of branding, on the Internet or elsewhere, is to burn your name in the mind. When you can successfully do that, there's no need for the prospect to use a search engine to find your Website. So in the long run, your Internet brand name will have to stand on its own. And a common name is a very weak foundation to stand on.

"Cars" is not a good name for an automotive dealership. And Cars.com is not a good name for a Website that sells cars. Neither is Mydiscountbroker.com a good name for a stockbroker on the Internet.

And what do you suppose Internet.com is all about? This is a brand that has two strikes against it. Internet.com is a common noun used for a Website that tries to appeal to everybody for everything. (You can hear the shouts of joy in the corridors at Internet.com. "Wow! We were able to register the best name on the Net." Don't be too sure.)

What's your own name? Brown, Jones, Smith? Would you consider changing your name to a generic? If you did, a phone conversation might sound like this:

"Hello, this is Some Person."

"I know that, but what's your name?"

In spite of our arguments to the contrary, there will be intense pressure inside every organization to take the common name route. It's the lemming effect. Once the crowd takes off in one direction, everyone just naturally joins in and follows. There's some psychological satisfaction in following the crowd. In art, in music, in clothing, and in Internet brand names.

"It is better for your reputation to fail conventionally," John Maynard Keynes once said, "than it is to succeed unconventionally."

Don't say we didn't warn you.

4

The Law of the Proper Name

Your name stands alone on the Internet,
so you'd better have a good one.

The torrent of generic brand names on the Internet provides hope for the late starters. If you can launch a Website with a good idea and a good brand name, you are in a good position. You can wait until the generic site names drop out of sight and then jump in and win big.

Make no mistake about it. Your name stands alone on the Internet and is by far your most valuable asset. This is one of the major differences between the Internet and the physical world.

In the physical world, there are many clues to a company's purpose. Location, window displays, even the size and architecture of the building. A hotel looks like a hotel, a bank looks like a bank, and a restaurant looks like a restaurant.

Even in the industrial field, you seldom are exposed to just the company's name. A brochure or direct-mail piece will usually have pictures that establish the company's product line or service.

On the Internet, however, the name stands alone. Until you

get to the site, you won't find any clues to what the site actually does.

In the physical world, a mediocre name can sometimes work because the physical clues combine to establish the company's identity. A watch store looks like a watch store.

The location and visual look of a retail store, for example, can be so unique that customers often forget the store's name. "It's the repair shop at the corner of 87th Street and York Avenue."

Even a droll name can work in a retail environment. "The Mattress Firm" for a bedding shop, for example. "The Money Store" for a home loan company. "General Nutrition Centers" for a health-supplement store. Names like these never stand alone. They always carry a wealth of clues that communicate their real purpose.

In the electronic world, there are no clues. There are no books in the window that tell you that Amazon.com is a bookstore. No travel posters that tell you that Priceline.com sells airline tickets. No greeting cards that tell you what Bluemountain.com does.

This is what leads Internet companies astray. Straight into the generic trap.

The lure of the generic is so powerful that some companies have paid enormous sums for names that in the long run will turn out to be useless. A Los Angeles company bought Business.com for $7.5 million. (To whom it may concern: If you had bought this book for $21, you would have saved yourself $7,499,979.00.) Some other recent purchases:

- Wine.com was bought for $3 million.

- Telephone.com was bought for $1.75 million.

- Bingo.com was bought for $1.1 million.

- Wallstreet.com was bought for $1.03 million.

- Drugs.com was bought for $823,456.

- University.com was bought for $530,000.

It's worse than tulip mania in Holland or truffle madness in France. The latest bid on the Loans.com name was $3 million. (If you own a common Internet name, our advice is to sell it before the mania melts away.)

Even at this early stage, the power of a proper name as opposed to a common name for an Internet brand has been clearly demonstrated. The big early winners (AOL, Amazon.com, eBay, Priceline.com, Yahoo!) have all been proper names rather than common names.

There's a lot of confusion on this issue. People see a name like Priceline and assume it's a common or generic name, but it's not. The generic name for the category is "tickets" or really "name-your-own-price airline tickets." Tickets.com is a common name used for a Website that, in our opinion, is not going to take off.

("Price" and "line" are common words, of course, but they are used out of context and in combination to create the proper name "Priceline," which becomes an effective Internet brand name.)

Every common name can also be a proper name if used to identify a single person, place, or thing. Bird is a common name, but it's also a proper name, as in Larry Bird or Tweety Bird.

When you are choosing a brand name for your Website, the first thing to ask yourself is, what's the generic name for the category? Then that's the one name you don't want to use for your site.

Invariably a singular proper name will turn out to be a better name for your site than a generic.

iVillage.com, for example, is a better name for a Website devoted to women than Women.com. (Yes, there is a Website called Women.com, and it's spending $10 million this year to promote its name.)

Ashton.com is a better name for a Website that sells luxury goods than Cyberluxury.com, eLuxury.com, or Firstjewelry.com.

In the physical world, the same branding principles apply. The proper name is superior to the common or generic name.

- McDonald's is a better name than Burger King.

- Hertz is a better name than National Car Rental. (All the car rental names you see in an airline terminal are national car rental companies, but there's only one Hertz.)

- *Time* is a better name than *Newsweek* or *U.S. News & World Report.*

- Kraft is a better name than General Foods, so when Kraft General Foods decided to simplify their name, they called the company Kraft and not General Foods.

There are degrees of commoness, of course. "Burger King" is not a totally common name. The Hamburger Place would be a totally common name for a fast-food establishment that features burgers.

There are degrees of properness, too. McDonald's and Hertz are more "proper" than *Time* magazine. *Time* is a common name used out of context to create a proper name.

In the same way, Amazon and Yahoo! are more "proper" than Priceline and eBay, which are common words used out of context. (All distinctions are relative, of course. Even Amazon and Yahoo! can be common words. A yahoo is a brutish creature and an amazon is a tall, vigorous, strong-willed woman.)

So how "proper" should your Website name be?

It all depends. First, and most important of all, you want your Website name to be perceived as a proper name. Then hopefully you want your name to be more "proper" than your competitors'. But you also want to consider other factors.

In addition to selecting a proper name, your Website naming strategy will be more effective if it is consistent with the following eight guidelines:

1. The name should be short.

In general, the shorter the better. Shortness is an attribute even more important for an Internet brand than an outernet brand.

You have to keyboard the Website name into your computer. That's why the site name should be both short and easy to spell.

Many Internet brands have two strikes against them. They

are both too generic and too long. As a result, they are hard to remember and hard to spell. Some examples:

- Artsourceonline.com.

- Dotcomdirectory.com

- eBusinessisbusiness.com

- Expressautoparts.com

- Interactivebrokers.com

- GiftCertificates.com

- OnlineOfficeSupplies.com

- Treasurechestonline.com

Starting with the generic name for the category and condensing it is a good way to kill two birds with one stone. You create a proper name that's also short and easy to spell. CNET.com, for example, took the generic term "computer network" and shortened it to CNET, creating a short, proper name that's also easy to spell.

Sandoz needed a brand name for its over-the-counter flu therapy product. So the company reversed the word order and condensed the name to TheraFlu. The product went on to become the leading brand in its category.

Nabisco needed a brand name for its vanilla wafers, so it called them Nilla. And the powerful brand name Jell-O is just a shortened version of gelatin dessert.

Nabisco itself is a brand name constructed by condensing

its former generic name, National Biscuit Company. (There are many national biscuit companies, but only one Nabisco.)

Barnesandnoble.com finally threw in the towel on their long, difficult-to-spell name and shortened it to bn.com.

Morgan Stanley Dean Witter is an enormously successful financial company, but Morganstanleydeanwitter.com is not going to make it on the Internet. The company shortened the name to msdw.com.

(The names bn.com and msdw.com are not good either, for reasons we will discuss under Immutable Law #9.)

The well-known consulting firm Booz Allen & Hamilton obviously couldn't use its long, complicated name on the Internet, so the firm launched Bah.com. (Not a particularly euphonious choice.) And what about names like Deloitte & Touche? Or PricewaterhouseCoopers?

The Internet will force many companies to take another look at their names. This is true even for companies for which the Internet is a medium and not a business. Instead of launching Bah.com, perhaps Booz Allen & Hamilton should have changed the consulting firm's name to Booz Allen and launched a site called BoozAllen.com.

And what about names like: Alleghany, Allegheny Teledyne, Allegiance, Anheuser-Busch, Bausch & Lomb, Canandaigua Brands, Di Giorgio, Harnischfeger, Hayes Lemmerz, Heilig-Meyers, Leucadia National, Marsh & McClennan, Phillips-Van Heusen, Rohm & Haas, Schering-Plough, Smurfit-Stone, Sodexho Marriott Services, Synovus Financial, Tecumseh Products, TIAA-CREF, Transmontaigne, Wachovia, Wackenhut, Weyerhauser.

All of these companies will have difficulty transferring their names to the Internet. And these are not small companies either. They are all ranked in *Fortune* magazine's list of the one thousand largest American companies.

Because of the Internet many companies will have to simplify their names. You have to misspell a name and address pretty badly before the Postal Service will refuse to deliver your letter. To reach a Website, however, you have to be perfect. You can't drop one of the periods or leave out a hyphen.

One way to have your cake and eat it too is by using both a name and a nickname on the Web. Charles Schwab is the leading discount brokerage firm, but on the Web the company uses both CharlesSchwab.com and Schwab.com, although it promotes only Schwab.com.

Ask Jeeves is one of the leading search-engine sites on the Internet, but it wisely operates with two site names: AskJeeves.com and Ask.com.

When you have to choose between several brand names that seem equally good, the smartest name to pick is usually the one that also has a good nickname.

People feel closer to a brand when they are able to use the brand's nickname instead of its full name.

- Beemer, not BMW

- Chevy, not Chevrolet

- Coke, not Coca-Cola

- Bud, not Budweiser

- FedEx, not Federal Express

- Mac, not Macintosh

2. The name should be simple.

Simple is not the same as short. Simplicity has to do with the alphabetical construction of the brand name. A simple word uses only a few letters of the alphabet and arranges them in combinations that repeat themselves.

Schwab is a short name (six letters), but it is not a simple name because it uses six letters of the alphabet. This is one reason that Schwab is not a particularly easy name to spell.

Mississippi is a long name (eleven letters), but it is also a simple name because it uses only four letters of the alphabet. Which is why most people can spell Mississippi.

Coca-Cola is both a short name and simple name. Although the name has eight letters, it is formed by using only four letters of the alphabet. Furthermore, the name repeats the "co" syllable.

Pepsi-Cola, on the other hand, is a much more complicated name than Coca-Cola. Pepsi-Cola uses eight letters of the alphabet to form a nine-letter word.

Autobytel.com, for example, suffers from the same problem. Like the Pepsi-Cola name, it takes eight letters of the alphabet to form the name. Furthermore, how do you "parse" the name? Is it Auto by Tel or Auto Bytel? And what is a Bytel anyway?

Even though the Autobytel Website has a proper name, along with an early lead in the car category, we don't believe it will become the premier site in its category.

Some people have criticized Nissan's decision to change its U.S. brand from Datsun to Nissan. But from a brand-name point of view, Nissan is the superior name. Although both brand names use six letters, the Datsun name requires six letters of the alphabet and the Nissan name only four. (You hardly hear anyone use the Datsun name anymore.)

3. The name should be suggestive of the category.

Here's the paradox. To become a big brand on the Web, you need a proper name. On the other hand, the name should suggest the category without falling into the generic name trap.

This is not an easy line to walk. Shortening the generic name is one way to achieve both objectives (CNET, Nilla, and Jell-O, for example).

Another approach is to add an "off-the-wall" word to the name of the category. PlanetRx, for example. (We would have preferred a different word than *planet,* which has been overused. In addition to the ailing Planet Hollywood chain, there are two other would-be planet brands on the Internet, Pet Planet and Planet Outdoors.)

DrugDepot.com might also have been a better name for an Internet drugstore than either Drugs.com or Drugstore.com.

It's alliterative and mimics both the Home Depot and the Office Depot brands in the physical world.

We helped a company that is planning to sell advertising specialties on the Web come up with the name BrandBuilders.com. (The company sells hats, T-shirts, pens, binders, and other material used in corporate brand-building projects.) Then we agreed with the client to shorten the name to Branders.com to make it more finger friendly.

4. The name should be unique.

Unique is the key characteristic that makes a name memorable. This is true for all brand names, especially those used on the Web. AskJeeves.com and JRKoop.com are two Internet brand names that are both unique and memorable.

No name, of course, is totally unique unless you create it from scratch, like Acura, Lexus, Kodak, or Xerox.

Ask Jeeves.com is associated with the butler and JRKoop.com with the former surgeon general of the United States. But these are singular individuals who are not going to be confused with the Websites that carry their names.

As a matter of fact, both individuals suggest the functions of their sites—Ask Jeeves for finding information and JR Koop for medical information.

But how unique is More.com, a site that is spending $20 million to tell you they sell health, beauty, and wellness products. Or MyWay.com or CheckOut.com or Individual.com or

Owners.com or YouDecide.com or Indulge.com or This.com or Respond.com. Or any of a hundred different sites being backed by millions of dollars' worth of venture capital and promoted with millions of dollars' worth of advertising.

A Waltham, Massachusetts, company is spending $20 million in television and radio advertisements to launch a gift-buying service called Send.com. How is anyone going to remember the name?

Let's say you wanted to buy a present for your friend Charlie for Christmas. Do you call Buy.com, Present.com, Gift.com, or what?

By definition a common or generic name is not unique. It does not refer to a specific person, place, or thing like a proper name does. Therefore, a common name used as a Website name for the generic category is not memorable.

5. The name should be alliterative.

Why do you think children move their lips when they read? They are converting the visual symbols represented by the letters and words into sounds that can be processed by their brains. The mind works with the sounds of words, not with their shapes.

When you grow up, you learn not to move your lips when you're reading. But this doesn't change the way your mind works. It still works with the sounds of words.

If you want people to remember something, rhyme it for them. "If the glove don't fit, you must acquit."

Frogdog.com is an improvement over the brand's original name, which was Sportsite.com.

Alliteration is another sure-fire way to improve your brand's memorability. Many real-world brand names are alliterative. Some examples:

- Bed, Bath & Beyond

- Blockbuster

- Big Bertha

- Coca-Cola

- Dunkin' Donuts

- Volvo

- Weight Watchers

In our search of active, well-promoted Internet brands, we could find none that used alliteration. (One of the reasons we liked BrandBuilders as a name was its alliteration.)

The same principle applies with babies. Give your newborn kid a head start. Pick a first name that's alliterative with your last name. It's a fact that many famous celebrities have alliterative names: Alan Alda, Ronald Reagan, Robert Redford, Tine Turner, Marilyn Monroe. One reason Bill Bradley is doing so well in his political campaign is his name. He has the best name of all the presidential candidates. It's doubly alliterative.

6. The name should be speakable.

When was the last time you bought something because you read an advertisement or a news item about it? Many people are hard put to remember a single item they bought because of an ad.

Does this mean that advertising is ineffective? Not necessarily. Most people buy products or services because they hear about these things from friends, neighbors, or relatives.

Word of mouth is the most effective medium in your entire communications arsenal. But how does the first mouth get the word to pass along? From publicity or advertising, of course.

As a rule of thumb, there are ten word-of-mouth recommendations for every publicity or advertising "hit." This ten-to-one ratio holds for many different products and categories.

As effective as word of mouth is, you can't build a brand by mouth alone. You have got to give that mouth something to work with. Unfortunately, too many companies use Internet brand names that are unspeakable. Many are common names that discourage word-of-mouth usage.

"Where did you buy your new computer?"

"It was Onsale."

"I know you got a good deal, but where?"

"Onsale."

Onsale.com might be a difficult name to use in ordinary conversation, but many other Websites are even worse. They're also hard to pronounce and spell. Some examples: Entrepreneur.com, Concierge.com, Cyberluxury.com, Onvia.com, imandi.com, Brodia.com, iWon.com, iOwn.com, Richoshet.com, zUniversity.com, Shabang.com, uBid.com, Cozone.com, Gift-Emporia.com, iParty.com, eHow.com, Travelocity.com, Adornis.com, 2Key.com.

When someone recommends a physical brand or a real-world retail store, you don't have to remember exactly how to spell the name. Is it Abercrombie & Fitch or Abacromby & Fitch? It doesn't matter in the mall; it does matter on the Web.

This is why an Internet brand should always try to line up all possible spelling variations of its name. 2Key and TwoKey, for example.

(Roughly 10 percent of the buying public suffers from some form of dyslexia. Why write off—or rather, spell off—the dyslexia market?)

Another problem is the mixing of letters and numbers. Very few outerbrands use both. (We could only think of 3M, 3Com, and 1-800-FLOWERS.)

Quite a few Internet brands, on the other hand, make this mistake: 1stBuy.com, 123greetings.com, 123tel.com, How2.com, Net2phonedirect.com, Pop2it.com, Click2Asia.com, Shop2-give.com, MP3.com, 4anything.com, 4charity.com, Fax4Free.com, Opus360.com, 800.com, 911gifts.com.

Why do most people find it easier to remember their phone number than their license plate number, even though they are both about the same length? Because license plates usually use both numbers and letters, which makes them much more difficult to recall. While the combination can sometimes make cute vanity plates (321GO), they make poor brand names.

And did you ever try to remember a Canadian postal code

like H3B 2Y7? A mixture of letters and numbers is usually much harder to recall than either letters or numbers alone.

One of the reasons that companies select unspeakable brand names has to do with the selection process.

Most brand names are selected visually, usually from a list of names printed on oversized sheets of white paper pasted on cardboard.

That's not the way prospects deal with brand names. They usually hear them verbally from friends, neighbors, relatives, and co-workers. Even the media exposure of brand names is heavily weighted to verbal rather than visual media. Nearly 90 percent of the average person's media time is spent listening to radio or television versus less than 10 percent reading newspapers or magazines.

In case you're wondering, the words you hear in a television commercial are far more likely to make an impression in your mind than the words you read on the screen. (The spoken word conveys emotion and secondary meanings, while the printed word just sits emotionless on the page or on the TV screen.)

When you select a brand name, you should listen to the proposed name being spoken, and not just stare at the word on a board. You can't hear capital letters or the sound of a circle ®. To be effective, a brand name needs to sound like a proper name or a word that conjures up a particular Website, not just a generic category.

7. The name should be shocking.

If you want prospects to remember your Internet brand, you need to make the name itself "shocking."

The best brand names have always had an element of shock or surprise. DieHard, the largest selling automobile battery, for example. Häagen-Dazs, the leading premium ice cream. EatZi's, the first gourmet take-out food chain. Diesel, the fashionable brand of jeans.

It's easy to go overboard and make the name so shocking that it offends people. FUBU is a brand name that comes close to the edge, although younger people are usually more tolerant of truly shocking names.

People sometimes ask us why we call our laws "immutable." Aren't some of your laws mutable? is a reasonable question. Maybe so, we reply, but to make it in the book business you need a shocking title. *The 11 Generally Accepted Laws of Internet Branding* is just not going to go anywhere at Barnes & Noble, Borders, or Amazon.com.

One of the most difficult tasks in public relations is getting a business book reviewed in the media. We're going to try as hard as possible, but the odds are that this book will probably be the eighth book we have written that will not be reviewed by the *Wall Street Journal*.

But the *Journal* did review a book entitled *Leadership Secrets of Attila the Hun*. Four hundred years from now, will the *25th Century Wall Street Journal* review a digital book entitled *Leadership Secrets of Adolf Hitler*? Could be.

An element of "shock" makes a name more memorable because it puts the power of emotion to work. To a certain extent, you remember events in your own life based on the degree of emotional involvement. Your graduation day, your wedding day, the day John F. Kennedy was shot.

You may have taken dozens of vacations in your lifetime, most of which remain in your mind as fuzzy memories. The vacations you will never forget, however, are the ones that contain strong emotional elements. An automobile accident, an overturned sailboat, the day you stepped on a bumblebee.

You see the same pattern on the Internet. Common names like Cooking.com and Furniture.com are bland and carry no shock or emotional involvement. They're hard to remember.

It's names that have a bit of bite to them that will turn out to be the better brand names on the Internet. Names like Yahoo! and Amazon.com. These are names that stir up some emotional response.

One good branding strategy for any Internet company is to immediately lock the "shocking" name into both the category and the benefit. Amazon.com has promoted itself as "Earth's biggest bookstore." This strategy works on several levels. The Amazon is the Earth's "biggest" river, and the alliteration of "biggest bookstore" makes the phrase more memorable.

If you don't lock your shocking name into either a category or a benefit, you waste the power of the name. We always thought that Prodigy was a good name for an Internet service provider, but not for a general site. Prodigy, in our opinion, should have been directed at children.

Other memorable Internet brand names are MotleyFool,

70

EarthLink, and MindSpring. Also Hotmail, the most popular free e-mail service, and Monster.com, the leading Website for job listings. Then there's WingspanBank.com, the new Internet bank being launched by Bank One.

8. The name should be personalized.

Obviously, every Internet brand cannot accommodate all of these eight naming strategies, including personalization. But when the situation allows it, you should consider naming your site after an individual.

This strategy has a number of advantages. First of all, it assures you a Website with a proper name rather than a common name. Second, it enhances the publicity potential of the site.

Many real-world brands have evolved from individuals. Ford, Chrysler, Chevrolet, Pontiac, Olds(mobile), Buick, Cadillac. Calvin Klein, Ralph Lauren, Tommy Hilfiger, Donna Karan, Liz Claiborne, L.L. Bean, Boeing, Forbes, Goodyear, Gillette, Heinz, Hertz, and Orville Redenbacher, to name a few.

Initially Dell Computer sold its products under the PC Limited brand name. But ultimately the company realized that the proper name (Dell) was much stronger than the generic name (PC Limited), so it was switched.

You enhance the publicity potential of a brand when you use the founder's name as the brand name. Look at all the publicity Michael Dell has received, publicity that directly benefits the brand. His competitor Mr. Compaq seldom gets mentioned.

And where would the Trump brands be without The Donald? Nowhere, because Donald doesn't like to spend money when he can get something for free. Don't knock PR. Donald Trump's whirlwind activities on behalf of his brands are what made them successful.

Brands are cold, silent, and lifeless. Only a person can articulate the brand's strategy, position, and objectives. The media want to interview people, not brands. And whenever possible, the CEO, not the brand manager.

You can't help it. If you are the CEO and you want your brand to become famous, you have to want to become famous, too. The most famous brands usually also have celebrity CEOs. Microsoft and Bill Gates. Sun Microsystems and Scott McNealey. Oracle and Larry Ellison. Apple and Steve Jobs.

Same on the Internet. AOL and Steve Case. Amazon.com and Jeff Bezos. Yahoo! and Jerry Yang and David Filo.

Simplify things. Make it easy for both your prospects and the media to associate the chief executive with the Website. Give them both the same name.

- J. R. Koop and JRKoop.com

- Michael Dell and Dell.com

- Charles Schwab and Schwab.com

It all starts with the name. If you pick a name that matches most of these eight naming strategies, then you will be well on your way to building a successful Internet brand.

5

The Law of Singularity

*At all costs you should avoid being
second in your category.*

There's **one big difference** between branding on the Internet and branding in the real world.

In the real world, there is always room for a number two brand.

- Duracell and Energizer

- Kodak and Fuji

- Hertz and Avis

- Nike and Reebok

- Exxon and Shell

There's a reason why number two brands can lead a healthy life on the outernet. They serve a need, not just for the consumer, but also for the trade.

Would a supermarket just stock Coca-Cola and not a second brand? No. The second brand gives the supermarket some leverage against the leader. "If Coca-Cola won't participate in our weekly promotion, we'll ask Pepsi-Cola."

The unspoken implication of every request made by the trade is, if you turn this deal down, we'll offer it to your competitor. The number two brand fills a real need in the trade.

Would airline terminal management sign an exclusive deal with Hertz, the leading car rental brand? Not if they wanted to have some leverage on the number of cars available for rent, the hours of service, the pricing, and so forth.

Say there's a McDonald's on the corner of a highly desirable fast-food site. The real estate developer across the street can't sell the site to Mickey D, so he or she turns to Burger King.

The airline terminal, the supermarket, the drugstore, the mall operator, even the real estate developer—all come between the customer and the brand. These middlemen, or the trade if you will, have a strong need for number two brands, even if the number two brand is essentially the same. It's not a product need. It's a leverage need.

You find a similar need in the industrial field; most companies insist on "a second source of supply." What if their primary supplier is out on strike? If a company didn't have a second source of supply for a particular part, it might have to shut down its production line.

"Nothing comes between me and my Calvins," Brooke Shields once said. On the Internet nothing comes between the customer and the brand. There are no middlemen, no trade, no real estate developers, no need for leverage against the leader. It's what Bill Gates calls "friction-free capitalism."

As a result, the Internet is more like a football game or a

political contest. It's the Law of Singularity. Second place is no place.

Or as a Nike television commercial once said about the Olympics, you don't win silver, you "lose gold." On the Internet, there are no silver or bronze medals.

On the Internet, monopolies will rule. There is no room on the Internet for number two brands. The Internet will operate more like the computer software industry, in which every category tends to be dominated by a single brand.

- In PC operating systems, it's Windows.

- In PC word-processing software, it's Word.

- In PC spreadsheet software, it's Excel.

- In PC presentation software, it's PowerPoint.

- In PC accounting software, it's Quicken.

Michael Mauboussin, chief investment strategist at Credit Suisse First Boston, found that Internet stocks adhere to a mathematical valuation system so rigid, it resembles patterns found in nature. The pattern suggests that there may be fewer ultimate winners than many investors expect.

As some sites get bigger, Mr. Mauboussin argues, they attract more users, and the more users they attract, the richer and more useful they become, attracting more users. This produces a "winner-take-all" outcome: a handful of Websites with almost all the business, and the rest with next to nothing; i.e., the Law of Singularity.

One of the many advantages of friction-free retailing is that there is no one in between the customer and the manufacturer taking their cut of the transaction. The price you pay for the lack of friction, however, is the virtual disappearance of the second brand.

For many products, it's the retailer that is responsible for the strength of the second brand. No retailer wants to be totally dependent on a single brand in each category. To do so would be to put the retailer at the mercy of the manufacturer. The second brand keeps the first brand honest.

For the most part, there seems to be a cordial relationship between manufacturers and retailers, but despite the surface friendliness, there are often deep disagreements about prices, payment terms, stocking fees, co-op advertising allowances, and return privileges. In the retail world, you don't fight fire with fire. You fight fire with a second brand.

On the Web the situation is different. The real world is the second brand. When Amazon.com offers best-sellers at 50 percent off, the book buyer mentally compares the Amazon deal with the 30 percent off one can find at most brick-and-mortar bookstores.

When Barnesandnoble.com (now bn.com) says "me, too," the prospect yawns. There just isn't any reason to switch, unless Amazon.com suffers a breakdown in service or pricing.

There's another reason why the Web puts the second brand under pressure. In the physical world, one brand's success creates a trend in the opposite direction. This is especially true for a fashion-oriented brand.

"No one goes there anymore," said Yogi Berra. "It's getting

too popular." Not as many people wear Ralph Lauren anymore either; it was getting too popular. Now everybody is into Tommy Hilfiger.

If it's Tommy today, you can be sure that tomorrow it will be somebody totally different. That's the power of the second brand approach.

But the Web lacks the visibility of the physical world. If everyone bought their books from Amazon.com, how would you know? It's this lack of visibility that mutes the backlash against a brand leader.

In reality, of course, there are many second brands on the Internet. Not only seconds, but thirds, fourths, fifths, and even sixths. In furniture for example, we have Behome.com, Decoratewithstyle.com, Dwr.com, Furniture.com, Furniture-Find.com, Furnitureonline.com, HomeDecorators.com, Home-Portfolio.com, Housenet.com, Living.com, and many more that we don't know about.

Does this mean that the furniture category is different from books? That the furniture category might have many brands, but that the book category will be dominated by one brand, presumably Amazon.com?

Not at all. It only means that there is no clear-cut furniture leader today. But tomorrow is another matter. In all likelihood, one furniture brand will get out in front of the pack and go on to dominate the category. What happened in books is likely to happen in furniture.

History sheds some light on this process. In 1910, there were 508 American automobile companies. Today there are just two: General Motors and Ford.

In 1985, there were almost a hundred companies making disk drives. Today, two companies, Quantum and Seagate, dominate the disk-drive market on a worldwide basis.

In 1990, there were some two hundred companies making personal computers. Today, two brands (Compaq and Dell) dominate the category.

In the real world, we call this process "the law of duality." In the long run, two brands will dominate the category, putting the third brand under enormous pressure.

- Compaq and Dell dominate the personal computer market, putting the IBM brand under pressure. IBM, which lost a billion dollars on PCs last year, recently announced that they would withdraw from the retail market.

- Coca-Cola and Pepsi-Cola dominate the cola market, putting the squeeze on the Royal Crown brand. RC Cola has been steadily losing market share.

- Kodak and Fuji dominate the photographic film market, virtually shutting out Agfa and driving the brand off the shelf.

It doesn't get any better for a brand buried in the pack. As time goes on, opportunities disappear. The leaders become more fixed in their positions. The longer a brand remains an also-ran, the less likely it is to catch up.

Substitute "singularity" for duality and you have a long-term picture of the Internet. Friction-free retailing has eliminated the function of the second brand.

Take books, for example. Will either Borders.com or

bn.com overtake Amazon.com? Unlikely, unless Amazon.com makes a major mistake.

Will either Borders.com or bn.com close the gap with Amazon.com? That's unlikely, too. What is far more likely to happen is that Amazon.com will increase its share of the online book market, putting severe pressure on both Borders.com and bn.com. The law of singularity at work.

But stay tuned. Amazon.com is in the process of making that major mistake that will open the door for its book competitors (see Immutable Law #9).

Is there any hope for a brand buried in second place? Of course there is. But the highest form of strategic thinking is to first look at your situation with a cold eye.

The impossible is impossible. If it's going to be impossible to make progress head-on against an Amazon.com, then you must back off and try a different approach.

What might that approach be? If the laws of branding are immutable (and we think they are), then you must do exactly the same thing that Amazon.com did. You must be first in a new category.

You can always create an opportunity to be first in a new category by narrowing your focus and by appealing to a segment of the market. It's as simple as that.

Instead of duplicating Amazon.com's site, a better strategy for Borders.com and bn.com would be to narrow the focus and specialize in a category of books. Business books, for example.

Which brings up the Law of Either/Or. If the Web is going to be a business for both Borders and Barnes & Noble, then

79

they need different names on their Websites. With the same names, it is harder to create identities on the Web that are distinct and different from their identities in the physical world. Line extension strikes again.

Actually a number of Internet companies are trying to compete with Amazon.com by doing exactly as we have just suggested, by narrowing their focus.

- Alibus.com in the used-book category.

- Medsite.com in the medical book category.

- Varsitybooks.com in the textbook category.

In each of these categories, of course, there are a number of other Internet brands. So which brand will be the winner in each category? It won't necessarily be the brand that was first in the marketplace. It won't necessarily be the brand that was first to become profitable. The winner will be the first brand to establish a dominant position in the prospect's mind. Then the Law of Singularity will take over and dampen the market shares of the runners-up. Nothing succeeds like success.

When building an Internet brand, you have to think category first and brand second. Customers are not primarily interested in companies, in brands, or even in Websites. They are primarily interested in categories. They are not primarily interested in buying a Volvo, for example. They buy a Volvo in order to get a safe car. Volvo is the leader in a mental category called "safe cars."

What's a Chevrolet? In truth, a Chevrolet is a large, small, cheap, expensive car or truck. One reason for the continuing decline of Chevrolet sales is the fact that General Motors has neglected to define the mental category that Chevrolet is supposed to occupy.

If you want to be the leader in a category, you first have to tell the prospect what the category is. Take a two-page advertisement from a recent issue of the *Harvard Business Review*. There were only fifteen words in the entire ad and here is every one of them.

> The internet is a blank canvas.
> You hold the brush.
> intendchange.com
> intendchange
> image • build • reinvent

Will the reader of this Intendchange.com advertisement have any idea what the category is? We doubt it. It will never hurt you to tell the reader exactly where to file your brand name in the mind. Books, auctions, travel, airline tickets, cosmetics, clothing, search engines, whatever.

"Earth's biggest bookstore" not only stakes out a category for Amazon.com, but also makes a strong claim for leadership in the category. "Image, build, reinvent" does neither.

In summary, don't get discouraged if you're not the dominant brand in a category. Just channel your branding efforts in a different direction. Just narrow your focus.

You can always create a powerful brand by narrowing the focus on the leader. The Internet is an enormous medium. The opportunities to narrow the focus are astronomical.

In the real world, many narrowly focused brands have been extraordinarily successful in competing with market leaders.

Back in the early eighties, IBM was the most powerful company in the world. It made the most money and had the best reputation. IBM was also the first company to introduce a serious 16-bit office personal computer, the IBM PC. So is IBM the leader in PCs today? No, Dell Computer is.

Unlike IBM, Dell makes only one product (personal computers) marketed to one segment (the business community) and sold through one distribution channel (direct to customers). Yet today Dell outsells IBM in personal computers. Less often yields much more.

What Dell did in personal computers, Sun Microsystems did in workstations. By focusing just on UNIX workstations, Sun built a powerful brand and an extremely profitable company. You don't have to have a full line to be successful.

When the Web matures, of course, there will be opportunities for number two brands. Until that day arrives, you need to be the leading brand in your category or look for an opportunity to narrow the focus in order to create a new category you can be the leader in.

6

The Law of Advertising

*Advertising off the Net will be a lot
bigger than advertising on the Net.*

Death and taxes used to be the only certainties in life.
Today you can add one more: advertising.

Advertising messages are ubiquitous. Everywhere you turn
you'll find an advertising message. From television to taxicabs
to T-shirts. From billboards to buses to bathrooms. (Now you
can't even take a leak without being exposed to advertising.)
In some circles, elevators are considered the next fast-rising
advertising medium.

Every major auto race, golf tournament, and tennis tournament has a corporate sponsor. All the bowl games are already
taken, from the Hooters Hula Bowl in Hawaii to the AT&T
Rose Bowl in Pasadena to the Nokia Sugar Bowl in New
Orleans.

Sports arenas around the country are rapidly selling their
names for advertising purposes. In San Francisco, Candlestick
Park is now 3Com Stadium. The Washington Redskins'
Landover Stadium is now FedEx Field. Internet companies are
also getting into the act. The Baltimore Ravens sold the naming

rights for their National Football League stadium to PSINet in a twenty-year deal for $93.5 million.

But the mother of all naming deals happened in Atlanta. Naming rights for the city's new basketball and hockey stadium were sold to Philips NV in a package deal estimated to be worth $200 million over twenty years. (The new Philips Arena cost only $140.5 million to build.)

When the name on the stadium is worth more than the physical stadium itself, you know that we live in an advertising-oriented world.

The traditional media, of course, have been saturated with advertising for as long as we can remember.

The average magazine is 60 percent advertising. The average newspaper is 70 percent advertising. But print media are at least partially supported by subscribers. Radio and broadcast television are almost totally supported by the advertising revenues they generate.

And they generate a lot of revenue. Last year alone advertisers spent $49 billion on broadcast TV advertising and $17 billion on radio advertising.

Cable television was once touted as the first ad-free communications medium, but that didn't last very long. Today cable TV is almost as saturated with advertising as regular TV.

With billions and billions of dollars chasing every available advertising medium, you can't blame the Internet folks for trying to tap into this treasure trove. The Internet was going to be another advertising medium, but bigger and better and eventually more rewarding than television.

Initially, at least, advertising supported all the commercial

Websites. The game plan was simple: "We will give away the content in order to draw traffic, which we can then use to sell advertising." Exactly the way television and radio currently work.

So we had free browsers, free search engines, free electronic mail, free electronic greeting cards, free Internet access. Even free phone calls and free tax returns.

Instead of paying America Online $21.95 a month, you can now sign up with Net Zero and get the same service for nothing. The catch: You must fill out a questionnaire that reveals your demographic information and agree to put up with an onslaught of advertising messages.

There's even free beer on the Net. Miller Brewing is giving away two million electronic coupons each good for one six-pack of any Miller beer brand.

The great Internet giveaway reached its zenith when a company called Free-PC announced a plan to give away ten thousand Compaq computers that permanently display on-screen ads. More than a million people volunteered to take one.

If "free" isn't a big enough come-on, how about "pay"? A number of Websites will reward you for exposing yourself to advertising while you surf the Net.

AllAdvantage.com will pay you fifty cents an hour (up to ten hours a month). MyPoints.com will give you either cash or points that can be exchanged for things like free movie rentals, gift certificates, ski-lift tickets, even exotic vacations. (Surf the Web today, surf Hawaii tomorrow.)

Many Websites feature giveaways of one kind or another. PlanetRx.com gave away 672 Palm V organizers (one an hour, every day, for four weeks). Lycos.com is a portal that offers a Lucky Numbers Game you can play up to four times a day. Just pick six numbers and cross your fingers. You could win one of 5,000 prizes, including a grand prize of $5 million.

The really big money is being thrown around by the CBS-backed Website iWon.com. The portal is giving away $10,000 a day, $1 million a month, and a cool $10 million on tax day, April 15, 2000. (Get it? I won.)

What the giveaway has to do with the Website remains a mystery. Unlike Youbet.com, iWon.com is not a gambling site. Rather, it is a portal that offers e-mail, search services, and online shopping, as well as content from CBS Websites including SportsLine USA and MarketWatch.com. All financed with $100 million of CBS money.

Besides the giveaways, many sites are spending a fortune on launch parties. Pixelon.com, a California company that plans to introduce a new Internet-broadcast technology, raised $23 million of venture capital and then promptly spent $10 million of that on a launch party. Called iBash '99, the day-long Las Vegas party was headlined by The Who, along with other acts that included Kiss, Natalie Cole, the Dixie Chicks, Tony Bennett, and LeAnn Rimes.

This flurry of spending is designed to attract millions of Web visitors who can then be sold off to companies as advertising chattel. As a matter of fact, Internet operators are drooling over the advertising riches soon to fall their way. Forrester Research, a high-tech consulting firm, predicts that advertising spending on the Internet will jump from $2 billion in 1999 to $22 billion in 2004, or 8 percent of total spending.

This would mean that the Internet passed the magazine medium and was neck and neck with radio.

Don't believe a word of it. The Internet will be the first new medium that will not be dominated by advertising.

Let us repeat that statement. The Internet will be the first new medium that will not be dominated by advertising, and the reason is simple.

The Internet is interactive. For the first time, the user is in charge, not the owner of the medium. The user can decide where to go, what to look at, and what to read. At many sites, the user can decide how to pick and arrange the material to best fit that user's needs.

Advertising is not something that people look forward to. They tend to have an underlying resentment toward advertising. They see it as an intrusion into their space, an invasion of their privacy. "Junk mail" is the popular term for direct-mail advertising.

(If magazines were interactive, the first thing readers would do is to put all the editorial material up front and all the advertising in the back.)

Initially, of course, people were curious about this new medium called the Internet. And they were happy to click on banner ads to see what all the buzz was about.

But things are changing. Surveys show that the number of people who click on Internet ads has been dropping steeply. According to Nielsen/NetRatings, which tracks the effectiveness of Internet advertising, the click rate in one year dropped from 1.35 percent to half that level.

Internet advertising rates have also been dropping, not a

sign of a healthy medium. According to one research firm, the cost for banner ads has dropped from $20 per thousand last year to about $10 per thousand this year.

The largest advertiser on the Internet last year was General Motors, which spent $12.7 million, or just one half of 1 percent of its total advertising budget of $2.12 billion. (All this advertising didn't help GM much. Its share of the domestic automobile market declined last year to 29.2 percent, its lowest level since the thirties.)

One indication of the Internet user's attitude towards advertising is the rapid rise of ad-blocking software. Known by names like At Guard, Junkbuster Proxy, Intermute, and Web Washer, these programs work by blocking ads before they appear on the user's screen. Often they speed up performance because the files that contain ads loaded with graphics are skipped, making page loading far quicker.

Even the $2 billion of current Internet advertising is a dubious number. It includes commissions paid to such companies as Doubleclick, the leading seller of advertising on the Net.

Doubleclick is aptly named. Instead of the traditional advertising agency's 15 percent commission, Doubleclick takes 35 percent to 50 percent of the Internet advertising it sells. Maybe Tripleclick would be a more appropriate name.

Not all Internet advertising revenues represent real money either. Some sites swap advertising with each other, allowing each dotcom to book ad revenues. (The kid who trades a $50,000 dog for two $25,000 cats isn't really receiving $50,000 in revenue.)

Don't be misled by the apparent analogies with the print

and broadcast media. The Internet is not just another medium. If it were, it would not be the revolutionary medium that many people, including us, believe it is going to be.

The Internet, in our opinion, is a revolutionary new medium. As such, you should expect to see a revolution, not just a replay of the past.

Was television a revolutionary new medium? Not really. Did it change your life in any significant way? Not really. Even television's highly touted home shopping networks didn't amount to very much. "Radio with pictures" was the judgment of many commentators.

You can't have it both ways. The Internet cannot be a revolutionary new medium that operates in exactly the same way as traditional media. Where's the revolution?

It's staring us in the face. The Internet is interactive, and that's the revolutionary aspect of the medium. For the first time the target is in charge, not the shooter. And what the target definitely does not want is more advertising arrows shot in its direction.

What people do want is information. Prices, sizes, weights, shipping dates, product comparisons. All presented in an interactive format.

We're not negative about advertising. Quite the contrary. The Internet has and will continue to spawn an enormous increase in advertising volume, except that it will be off the Net rather than on the Net. This advertising will be "tune-in"—or rather "type-in"—advertising that will direct you to the names of specific Internet sites.

The Internet has already driven up advertising on the outernet, especially on radio and television. TV advertising revenues were up 4 percent last year and radio advertising revenues were up 12 percent. Anybody who watches television or listens to radio has to have noticed the sharp increases in Website commercials. (Radio, in particular, is red-hot, with three years of double-digit increases in a row.)

"The purpose of a dotcom," jokes Michael Murphy, "is to transfer money from venture capitalists to advertising agencies."

Super Bowl Sunday has become a particular favorite of Internet advertisers. Of the 36 companies that bought advertising time on Super Bowl XXXIV, 17, or almost half, were dotcoms. The NFL extravaganza doesn't come cheap either. The average cost for a thirty-second commercial was more than $2 million, an increase of 25 percent over Super Bowl XXXIII.

While Internet advertising rates have been declining, outernet advertising rates have been climbing sharply. (There's only so much broadcast time available.)

The reason the Internet has resulted in dramatic increases in outernet advertising has to do with the nature of the human mind.

One of the most remarkable characteristics of the human mind is its ability to forget. A computer never forgets. An airplane crashes with two hundred people on board and the nation is horrified. Does this hurt the airline's reputation? In the short term, yes, but in the long term, no. People forget.

Does American Airlines have a better safety record than United or Delta? Who knows, except executives of those three airlines?

Some things are never forgotten. A cruel insult in high school. Getting dumped by a lover. Being fired from a job. It all depends on the emotional impact of the event.

A person who can remember all the details of an embarrassing event that happened several decades ago might easily forget the underwear brand they put on this morning.

An Internet brand suffers from this ability of the mind to forget in two different ways. First, the brand is invisible on a daily basis. Many brands in the physical world benefit from a daily dose of visual reinforcement. Shell. Starbucks. Mobil. Coca-Cola, McDonald's, Tylenol. There are literally thousands of brands that a person will regularly see on the highways, in the supermarkets, in the drugstores.

An Internet brand, on the other hand, will never suddenly appear before you unless you summon it to do so. Out of sight, out of mind.

Second, an Internet brand (like most brands) suffers from a lack of emotional involvement. Some people fall in love with their brands. Most do not.

For most people a brand is nothing more than a guarantee of quality and a system for saving time. A way of making sure that the products you buy are decent without having to spend an inordinate amount of time comparing one product with another. Not too many people fall in love with a bottle of Heinz ketchup. Which is why Heinz needs the visibility on supermarket shelves and restaurant tables to keep the brand alive.

What does an Internet brand need to do to stay alive? It also needs visibility in the real, or physical, world.

The best and most cost-effective way to achieve visibility is with publicity. The first brand in a new Internet category is generally blessed by a blizzard of publicity. Amazon.com, Priceline.com, and Bluemountain.com are prime examples.

Some sites are capable of generating publicity on a continuing basis. The crazy auctions that happen every day on eBay are an endless source of stories. A recent headline in the *National Enquirer:* "He buys $3 pickle jar at garage sale & sells it for $44,000." (On eBay, naturally.)

The Internet itself will spawn an enormous increase in PR activity. "Just as network TV built the advertising business," says Ray Gaulke, president of the Public Relations Society of America, "the Internet technology has the capacity to dramatically build the PR business."

Sooner or later, however, many Internet brands will exhaust their publicity potential. At this point they will need to shift their emphasis from publicity to advertising. How else are you going to keep an invisible Internet brand alive?

Publicity first, advertising second is the general rule, and it applies to all branding programs, especially for Internet brands. (A much more detailed discussion of the relationship between publicity and advertising is contained in our previous book, *The 22 Immutable Laws of Branding.*)

As the Internet grows up, you are going to see an explosion in outernet advertising. And much of this advertising will be directed at creating customers for Internet brands.

In particular, radio will turn out to be the primary medium for dotcom advertising. Radio's perceived negative, the lack of visuals, is not a disadvantage for an Internet brand. There are no visual attributes of an Internet brand. No yellow flesh that helps identify Perdue chicken. No radiator grills that do the same for Mercedes-Benz automobiles. The only thing your mind needs to remember to log on to a site is the name.

On the Internet the name is everything. A verbal medium like radio is perfect for driving an Internet name into the mind. In summary, advertising might be vitally important for driving prospects to your site, but once they get there you can forget about using them as human fodder for your advertising messages.

On the Internet, interactivity is king. Advertising is something that prospects put up with, not something they search out. Interactivity gives them a choice, and in our opinion most people will use this choice to turn off the advertising and turn on the information.

If you want to build a brand on the Net, forget about trying to attract advertising to your Website.

Make your brand a source of information that prospects cannot find elsewhere. Or a place to buy things they cannot find elsewhere. Or a place to buy things at prices they cannot find elsewhere. Or a place to meet people they cannot meet elsewhere.

Don't make your site an excuse to run advertising that people have already seen in newspapers and magazines or heard on radio or TV.

The Internet is a revolutionary new interactive medium. And when people interact with advertising, they generally turn it off.

7

The Law of Globalism

*The Internet will demolish all barriers,
all boundaries, all borders.*

One of the major factors driving the global economy of the nineties was the collapse of communism in the late eighties. Instead of a world divided into armed camps, everybody was suddenly in the same boat.

Instead of trading insults, the major countries of the globe started to trade products and services.

But what caused the fall of communism? In our opinion, it wasn't the massive military buildup in the West, although that might have been necessary for defensive purposes. In our opinion, it was television.

If you visited the USSR before its fall, you know that the population was under intense publicity pressure to believe that everything was superior in the Union of Socialist Soviet Republics. Free health care, jobs for all, housing for everybody.

To the outsider, it wasn't true. There were a lot of rubles, but nothing to buy, as one look at the mostly empty shelves in the stores should have told you. Not to mention the long line whenever a store got a shipment of a desirable item.

Soviet authorities, of course, blocked Western newspapers and magazines from crossing their borders, but they couldn't block Western television signals.

Television brought truth to the Soviet people. When they were able to see the profusion of goods and services in the Western countries, they lost their faith in communism.

"The medium is the message" is the famous dictum of Marshall McLuhan. If you define "message" simply as "content" or "information," McLuhan pointed out, you miss one of the most important features of any medium: its power to change the course and functioning of human relations and activities.

The message of the television medium was "capitalism." As long as the Soviet Union was infiltrated by television signals from the West, there was no way to keep communism alive. It had to give way to a market-driven economy based on a free enterprise system. TV literally helped change the course of human history.

What is the "message" of the Internet medium? We believe the message is "globalism." Ultimately, the Internet will drive the citizens of the world into one interconnected global economy. "The global village," in McLuhan's vocabulary.

It may well be that the biggest trend of the twenty-first century will turn out to be globalism. What the Internet hath wrought is the global village. The medium is the message.

America, with 37 percent of all homes connected, is the dominant dog in Internet usage. But other countries are catching up. Finland has 23 percent of all households connected. Sweden, 18 percent. The United Kingdom, 14 percent. Europe as a whole, 9 percent.

Internet usage in Japan has almost doubled in the past year, from 6 percent to 11 percent. If our domestic experience is any guide, usage should explode in every developed country of the world. When that happens, the world will become one big global marketplace.

The potential is awesome. America is by far the largest economy in the world with the greatest output of goods and services and the highest standard of living. Yet the United States accounts for less than 5 percent of the world's population, a percentage that declines annually.

If you're a businessperson in America, where does the real opportunity lie? In the domestic market or in the 95 percent of the world that doesn't live in one of the fifty states?

Obviously the global market is going to be far more important than the domestic market to the success of almost every American company. It won't happen overnight, but it will happen.

There's a long way to go. Currently the United States exports only 20 percent of its gross national product. (It also exports capital to other countries, where the money is used to build plants, distribution systems, and most important of all, brands.)

What makes the American economic system so globally powerful is not the physical products or the plants or the systems, it's the brands themselves: Microsoft, Intel, Dell, Cisco, Coca-Cola, Hertz. These and other American brands dominate a host of categories on the worldwide scene.

This is not a one-way street, however. The Internet is not just an opportunity to export American brands and American

97

cultures overseas. The opposite is also likely to happen. It's already happened in many categories.

• While McDonald's has carried American fast food around the world, the truth is that a large number of Americans are eating Italian, Mexican, Chinese, French, and Japanese food.

• While Disney has just signed a deal for a new theme park in Hong Kong, the truth is that the most popular characters among the kiddie crowd in America are not Mickey Mouse or Donald Duck. They're Pokémon characters from Japan.

• Starbucks is a European-style coffee house blended with an American brand name.

• Evian from France started the trend toward branded bottled water, which has become an enormous category in the United States.

• Volkswagen and Toyota started the trend toward small cars in America.

• Mercedes-Benz and BMW from Germany started the trend toward small ultraluxury cars in the U.S.

• At the high end of the market, wine from France, watches from Switzerland, and clothing from Italy have had a major impact in the American market.

America has always been a melting pot for people, but it has also become a melting pot for products from around the world. With the rise of the Internet, that trend is going to accelerate. The medium is the message.

Many Websites here in America already do a considerable amount of business outside the United States. With the purchase of two European competitors, Amazon.com has become the leading online bookseller in the UK and Germany. Sales outside the United States currently account for 22 percent of Amazon's sales.

This is a drop in the bucket. The potential is much, much greater. What the postal service did for the Sears, Roebuck catalog, the Internet will do for the American business community. Or, for that matter, any business operating in any country anywhere in the world. The Internet turns the world into one giant shopping mall.

But like in any shopping mall, you can't win with just a better product or service. You need a better brand.

The long-term winners on the Internet will be those brands that can transcend borders. This is another knock on generic names.

What does Furniture.com mean in South America? It certainly doesn't mean *muebles,* the Spanish word for furniture. Or *mobiliário,* the Portuguese word for the same thing.

Amazon.com means *books* in virtually every country of the world. But Books.com means *books* only in the 5 percent of the world where English is the native language.

As the world moves toward a global marketplace, won't companies need to get rid of their national identities and move toward brands with global identities?

Not necessarily. Every brand, including global brands, needs to come from somewhere. In other words, even a global brand needs a national identity.

- Burger King is a global brand with an American identity.

- Volvo is a global brand with a Swedish identity.

- Rolex is a global brand with a Swiss identity.

Like a person, every brand needs to come from somewhere. No matter where the brand is made, marketed, or sold.

A Nissan made in America by American workers is still a Japanese brand of automobile. A Nike made in Malaysia by Malaysian workers is still an American athletic-shoe brand.

What's more important, the product or the brand? The fact that a product can maintain a national identity when the product in question has never set foot in that country should tell you that the brand is more important.

Global brand builders should keep in mind that national identity is a two-edged sword. It can help or hurt your brand, depending upon the category.

American personal computers (built in Asia or with Asian parts) are powerful brands on the global marketplace. American automobiles, no matter where they are built, are mediocre brands everywhere except in America.

What the global market is telling us is that Americans know how to build computers but don't know how to build cars. Is it true? It doesn't matter. When it comes to building brands, perception is more important than reality.

It's hard enough to change the perception of a company. It's impossible for one company to change the perception of a country. When you launch your Internet brand, you should try to match your product or service with your country's perception.

- If we wanted to set up a clothing site on the Internet, we would probably move to Italy and give the site an Italian name.

- If we wanted to sell wine on the Net, we would move to France.

- If we wanted to sell watches on the Net, we would move to Switzerland.

At least that's the theory. In practice it's different. Knowing something about government regulations for wine in France, we would probably choose Chile or Australia instead.

Don't overlook the less developed countries of the world. These nations represent tremendous opportunities for global brand builders wherever they are located. In the less developed countries, retail margins are often higher, fewer products are available, and even fewer products are on display.

For people in some of these countries, many Internet sites will look like the Sears, Roebuck catalog at Wal-Mart prices.

Is it unfair to take advantage of people in developing nations? If offering a better selection of better products at lower prices is unfair, then we don't know the meaning of the word.

Shipping the products (or perhaps we should say "flying" the products) isn't going to be the problem you might think it is. The postal service will airmail a copy of the book you are reading to an address in Indonesia for less than $10, which is about the retail margin of this book in a domestic bookstore. And costs are bound to come down dramatically as globalism catches fire and demand for air shipments soars.

101

One real barrier to globalism is red tape—taxes, duties, customs forms, and paperwork in general. These are the things that are going to clog up the system and slow it down. But you can't stop progress. In time, the paper barriers will come down, too.

Another barrier to globalism is language. The first decision a global brand builder must make is the language question. Do you use English, or do you translate your site into various different languages? Do you set up totally different sites for different countries? (Yahoo! launched Yahoo! en Español in 1998 and Yahoo! Brazil in 1999.)

The translation problem can be daunting. How many different languages and/or countries sites should you develop? There are literally thousands of languages in use by the 6 billion people in the world. If you count only the languages used by a significant number of people (say a million or more), there are still 220 different languages. To be a truly global brand, you would need Websites in a substantial percentage of those 220 languages.

Complicating this decision is a long-term trend toward English as the second language of the world. In many countries of the world, English is already the language of business.

(The Scandinavian region of a European company, for example, will inevitably hold its meetings in English. Few representatives from Norway, Sweden, Finland, and Denmark can speak any of the other languages, but they all know English.)

In the long term you are likely to find successful examples of both single-language and multiple-language sites. Either strategy can work. It all depends upon the type of product or the type of service offered.

For high-tech products and services or for brands appealing to the high-end segment of the market, the single-language strategy might be best. Cisco.com is an example.

For low-tech products and services or for brands appealing to the mainstream market, a multiple-language strategy might be best. Yahoo! en Español is an example.

(While the thinking at Yahoo! is sound, the strategy is flawed. The line extension name creates the impression that Yahoo! en Español is not an authentic brand. Rather, it's a gringo brand in disguise.)

Keep in mind, however, a basic tenet of marketing: There is never only one way to do anything. Most people prefer brands, but there is still a market for private labels. Most people prefer specialty stores, but there still is a market for department stores. Most people prefer caffeinated cola, regular beer, and coffee, but there is still a market for decaffeinated cola, light beer, and tea.

Whichever language decision you make, you can be sure there will be at least one competitor going in the opposite direction. So be it. You can't appeal to everyone. There is never only one way to do anything.

If you must err, however, err on the side of an English-only site. It will seem more upscale and chic. Time will also be on your side. Every day more than ten thousand people in non-English-speaking countries learn to speak the English language. Furthermore, English is the language of more than 80 percent of the information stored on computers.

There is also a worldwide trend toward the use of English-sounding brand names, even when those brands are sold primarily in non-English-speaking countries.

- *Hollywood* is a brand name for a Brazilian cigarette and also for a French chewing gum.

- *Montana* is a brand name for a Mexican cigarette.

- *Red Bull* is a brand name for an Austrian energy drink.

- *Boxman* is a brand name for a Swedish online music company.

- *StarMedia* is a brand name for a Spanish- and Portuguese-language Web portal.

Take a walk down the main shopping street of almost any major city in the world. A substantial number of locally owned stores selling locally made goods mostly to local people will have English names.

In Copenhagen, for example, we noticed that about half the stores on the main shopping street use English names. Some of these are franchise operations like McDonald's, Subway, and Athlete's Foot. But most are locally owned stores with names like Inspiration, Planet Football, and London House.

In a Tel-Aviv mall, we noticed five stores in a row with the following names: Gold Shop, Happy Tie, Happytime, Royalty, and Make Up Forever.

The trend to English names will obviously benefit all U.S. brands. Before you decide to go with a multiple-language approach, ask yourself whether this trend will make a single-language (English) approach your best overall choice for the future.

Some people think that globalism will be more of a cultural problem than a language problem. That you have to adapt your product or service to the cultures of the countries you are going to sell in. We disagree.

How did Coca-Cola, McDonald's, Levi Strauss, and Subway adapt their brands to local cultural standards? They didn't, and they greatly benefited because they didn't.

The medium is the message. And the message is the homogenization of cultures around the world. That's what globalism is all about. That's neither good nor bad. That's a fact.

When StarMedia was trying to raise capital to launch the first global Internet portal in Spanish and Portuguese, the company got the usual arguments.

"Latinos like to have personal contact with each other. Nobody's going to chat online. People want to talk on the phone. Latin Americans are so different from each other, no Argentine will ever want to talk to somebody from Peru."

StarMedia, of course, became a roaring success. Latinos did learn to chat online. People are more alike than different, even though the culture crowd likes to pretend otherwise.

Globalism has benefited from a number of technological developments, notably the jet plane and the facsimile machine. But these developments pale in comparison with the changes the Internet will bring.

So fasten your seat belts and get ready for the ride of your life.

105

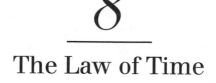

The Law of Time

*Just do it. You have to be fast. You have
to be first. You have to be focused.*

Haste makes waste, but waste is often the most important ingredient in a successful Internet launch.

If you want to be successful in business . . . in branding . . . in life . . . you have to get into the mind first. Notice we said "mind," not "marketplace."

Being first in the marketplace doesn't buy you anything except a license to try to get in the mind first. If you throw away that opportunity by being too concerned with getting all the details right, you'll never get it back. (Perfection in infinite time is worth nothing.)

What many managers are calling "the first mover advantage" is a myth. There is no automatic advantage to being the first mover in a category unless you can make effective use of the extra time to work your way into the prospect's mind.

A strategy that many large companies use effectively is to quickly jump on an idea developed by a smaller company. With its greater resources, the larger company can often win

107

"the battle of the mind" and create the perception that it was first in the marketplace.

If you are the CEO of a smaller company, beware. You need to move exceptionally fast. Be quick or be dead. Marketplace Darwinism is survival of the fastest.

First in the mind doesn't mean "early" in the mind either. Too many companies are satisfied with being "one of the first" brands in the category. That's not the same as getting into the mind first and creating the perception that you are the leader.

- Yahoo! was introduced in 1994 as the first search engine on the Internet. Today Yahoo! is the leading search engine and second only to AOL in the rankings of most-visited Websites.

- eBay was introduced in 1995 as the first auction site on the Internet. Today eBay is by far the leading auction site on the Net, handling more than 2 million auctions a month in some 850 product categories.

- Amazon.com was introduced in 1995 as the first bookstore on the Internet. Currently the company sells a billion dollars' worth of books a year, many times that of its nearest competitor, Barnesandnoble.com. Jeff Bezos, Amazon.com's founder, was named *Time* magazine's person of the year for 1999.

- Bluemountain.com was introduced in 1996 as the first electronic greeting-card site. Currently the site receives 10 million unique visitors a month, more than all its competitors combined. Recently the site was sold to Excite At Home for $780 million.

- Priceline.com was introduced in 1998 as the first company to sell airline tickets on the Internet with a "name-your-own-price" bidding system. Today Priceline.com is far and away the leading site on the Web for discount airline tickets and hotel rooms. Every seven seconds, someone names their own price at Priceline.com.

Five companies, five brands, five Internet "firsts." And five market leaders whose brands dominate their categories.

Were Yahoo!, eBay, Amazon.com, Bluemountain.com, and Priceline.com literally first in their categories? It's hard to know for sure, but probably not.

What you can be sure about is that the ideas for these sites occurred to many other people at about the same time. History shows that ideas tend to arrive in a variety of minds at approximately the same time.

The automobile was "invented" in Germany at about the same time as entrepreneurs in France, England, Italy, and America were working on many of the same self-propelled concepts.

The airplane was "invented" in America, but many French people thought the airplane was invented in France until they read about the Wright brothers accomplishing the same feat several years earlier.

Would we still think the world is flat if it weren't for Christopher Columbus? Of course not. Somebody else would have discovered America and realized the world was round.

Would we still be communicating with smoke signals if it weren't for Alexander Graham Bell? Of course not. Somebody else would have invented the telephone.

Would we still be using Thermofax copiers if it weren't for

Chester Carlson? Of course not. Somebody else would have invented xerography.

There's a big difference between having an idle thought on a Sunday afternoon and having a successful brand on the Internet on Monday morning. Ideas (and those idle thoughts that initiate them) are a dime a dozen. It takes hard work and, even more important, a sense of urgency to put an idea to work on the Net.

You can't dawdle. By this we mean endless testing, focus groups, market surveys. This is a particular problem for an Internet brand.

Why were most of the successful Internet sites launched by small, venture-capital-backed companies rather than *Fortune* 500 firms? A big company hates to do anything without first amassing a mound of market research.

The Internet is moving too fast to be measured. It's a new industry. Knowledge is scarce. Few people know what they want, what they would use, what they would be willing to pay for . . . until they are given a real-world choice.

Big companies often fail to exploit new opportunities because they are "perfectionists." They won't release a new product, a new service, or an Internet site "until we get it right."

Getting it right makes no sense from a branding point of view. Anything worth doing is worthwhile doing in a half-assed way. Anything not worth doing is not worth doing in a perfect way.

Take Yahoo!, the most valuable brand on the Internet. Yahoo! is basically a search engine. It will find whatever you want to find on the Internet.

Did Yahoo! develop its own search-engine technology? No. In order to move rapidly, it outsourced its search-engine technology, first from Open Source, then from AltaVista, before finally settling on Inktomi.

The leading search engine didn't develop its own search-engine technology? Does that surprise you? It shouldn't. You don't win by being better. You win by being first. Yahoo! succeeded because they "rushed the net."

One of the abiding myths of American business is that you win by being better. Management commits billions of dollars in their search for better products or services to market. They "benchmark" their existing products and services against their major competitors. No new product or service gets launched unless it has a significant, tangible advantage.

Result: Nine out of ten new products fail. Why? Not, in our opinion, because of a quality deficiency. It's because of a timing deficiency. They didn't get that new product or service out in the marketplace fast enough.

Big companies often lack a sense of urgency when it comes to introducing new products or new ideas. Sometimes you can detect that sometimes in their public statements. "Maybe we are relatively late," said Rupert Murdoch, CEO of News Corp. when he recently announced the company's first Internet investment, "but only by a year or two."

Only by a year or two? In less than two years, Priceline.com went from nothing to market leadership of a new category on the Internet. Market value: $7.9 billion.

Carpe diem. Where would Microsoft be today if Bill Gates didn't drop out of Harvard in his freshman year to go to

Albuquerque, New Mexico, to develop an operating system for the world's first personal computer?

Carpe diem. Where would Dell Computer be today if Michael Dell hadn't dropped out of the University of Texas in his sophomore year to start a company selling computers directly to business.

Carpe diem. Today is the best day of your life to launch an Internet company based on a new idea or concept. One that nobody else is using.

Another reason for haste is the stock market. The unbelievable success of Internet stocks has driven investors crazy. Nobody wants to miss the financial opportunity of a lifetime. Money is available, but time is not. There are stacks of cash waiting for any twenty-five-year-old with a half-baked idea. The competition that a brand of car, cola, or cookie might face is nothing like the bewildering array of brands on the Net. If you want to capture your share, you must act rapidly and you must act now.

Have you ever heard of NorthernLight.com? You're not alone. More than 99 percent of Web users are not familiar with the site.

Northern Light Technology LLC is the largest search engine on the Internet, in the sense that it indexes some 160 million Web pages. That's far more than Yahoo!, Excite, Lycos, or Infoseek. Plus Northern Light compiles the contents of some six thousand full-text sources such as business magazines, trade journals, medical publications, investment databases, and news wires.

The problem is not the site. The problem is the timing.

112

Northern Light didn't get turned on until three years after the Yahoo! launch. That's much too late. Not only was Yahoo! gathering momentum, but the new search site also had to compete with AltaVista, Excite, Infoseek, and Lycos.

The problem is not the money. Northern Light was financed with $50 million in venture capital, far more than Yahoo! had to work with.

It's bad enough to start in second place. It's worse to start at the back of the pack. In many situations it's almost hopeless.

So what do you do if you're late? Too many managers put on their Avis hats and say "We have to try harder." Not good enough. (Remember the Law of Singularity.)

Paradoxically, it's never too late. But you can't launch in the year 2000 a great idea, circa 1995. If you get into the game late, you have to narrow your focus. Michael Dell was late, very late, into personal computers. So he decided to focus on selling personal computers by telephone. A good strategy. Today Dell Computer is the world's second largest manufacturer of personal computers.

Michael Dell didn't make the same mistake when the Internet arrived. His company was the first to sell personal computers on the Web. Also a good strategy.

Nor is it ever enough just to move rapidly without a basically good idea. Time Warner was one of the first companies to set up an Internet site. Hence the name, Pathfinder.

But what's a Pathfinder? At first the site was nothing more than a collection of information pulled from various Time Warner magazines: *Time, People, Fortune, Money, Entertainment Weekly,* and others. After the purchase of Turner

113

Broadcasting System, the company added CNN, CNNsi and CNNfn to the site. They even managed to sell American Express on listing *Travel & Leisure* magazine on the site as well as *AsiaWeek,* a Hong Kong publication.

After investing a reported $75 million in the site, Time Warner recently shut it down. What's a Pathfinder? The only meaning the name had was that it was a site for Time Warner publications. But few people care who publishes a magazine (unless John F. Kennedy Jr. is involved, and now that he is gone, *George* magazine is in grave trouble). They only care about the magazine itself.

Nobody reads *Fortune* because Time Warner publishes it. They read *Fortune* in spite of the fact that Time Warner publishes it. The name of the company that publishes the magazine is irrelevant to the average reader. *Fortune* is the brand, not Time Warner.

After Time Warner gave up on Pathfinder, the company retreated to individual sites for each of its major publications. Also not a good strategy. (Line-extension sites of magazine brands might be good for selling a few subscriptions, but they are not the way to build a powerful presence on the Web.)

Time Warner bills itself as the "world's foremost media company." How could two yahoos from Stanford beat the world's foremost media company?

Easy. All you need to do is to get your strategy right and your timing right. Both are required. One without the other won't work.

P.S.: You probably noticed that it was AOL that took over Time Warner and not vice versa.

9

The Law of Vanity

*The biggest mistake of all is
believing you can do anything.*

Success in business doesn't just show up on the bottom line of the profit-and-loss column; it also goes to the top. Success in business inflates the egos of top management.

Supremely successful companies believe they can do anything. They can launch any product into any market. They can make any merger work. It's just a question of having the willpower and the resources to throw into the task. "What is it that we want to do?" is the question that management usually asks itself.

History hasn't been kind to this type of thinking. Overconfident management has been responsible for most of the marketing disasters of the past decades.

- General Electric couldn't crack the mainframe computer market in spite of its reputation for brilliant management.

- Sears, Roebuck's "socks and stocks" strategy of selling brokerage accounts, insurance, and real estate in its retail stores went nowhere.

- Xerox couldn't duplicate its copier success in computers.

- IBM, on the other hand, couldn't extend its computer success to copiers.

- Kodak lost its focus when it tried to get into instant photography.

- Polaroid, on the other hand, fared no better in conventional 35mm film.

Get the picture? As soon as a company is successful in one area, it tries to move into another. Usually with little or no success.

The problem is usually not the new product or service being offered. Xerox may well have had the best computer product on the market. The problem is in the mind of the prospect. "What does a copier company know about computers?"

In other words, the problem is not a product problem, it's a mental problem. The most difficult problem in business is trying to change a perception that exists in the mind of a customer or prospect. Once a perception is strongly held in the mind, it can almost never be changed. (Anybody who has ever been married knows the difficulty of changing a perception in another person's mind.)

What's a Cadillac? In the mind of the car buyer, it's a "big car." But the market started shifting to smaller cars. So naturally Cadillac tried to sell a small Cadillac called the Catera, with very little success.

What's a Volkswagen? In the mind of the car buyer, it's a "small car." But its customers now have families. So naturally

Volkswagen tried to sell a larger Volkswagen called the Passat, with very little success.

Cadillac couldn't sell small Cadillacs. And Volkswagen couldn't sell big Volkswagens.

Once you stand for something in the prospect's mind, it's hard to change what you stand for. Volkswagen stands for small. Cadillac stands for big. Can you change these perceptions? (And, furthermore, why would you want to?)

Unlikely. Yet they keep trying. Before the Catera launch, Cadillac tried selling the Cimarron, another smaller Cadillac. Predictably the Cimarron also never got out of the garage.

The folks at Lincoln ought to be laughing at Cadillac's predicament, but they're not. They too are busy introducing the new small Lincoln (LS for Lincoln Small, of course).

Meanwhile the three-and-a-half-ton Lincoln Navigator is doing great. When a new product matches the perceptions that already exist in the mind, the new product can be exceedingly successful.

When Volkswagen brought back the Beetle, their original small car, sales exploded. As you might expect, the success of the New Beetle also went to their heads. "There's no reason we can't sell $80,000 cars with the Volkswagen name on them," said one VW executive recently. Yes, there is. People won't buy them.

Will the online world be any different than the off-line world? We think not. To be successful on the Internet you still have to do business with human minds. Once you stand for something in a mind, it's hard to change the perception of what you stand for.

117

Amazon.com was the first Internet site to sell books and music CDs. The site is a roaring success, with current sales well in excess of $1 billion annually (albeit with losses in the past year in the $300 million range).

So what is Amazon.com doing next? You know what they're doing next. They're in the process of turning themselves into a "destination site" where customers can find anything they could possibly want.

- DVDs and videotapes.

- Electronics and software.

- Toys and video games.

- Home improvement products.

- A gift-registry system.

- E-cards.

- Auctions, including a joint venture with Sotheby's (Amazon spent $45 million for a 1.7 percent stake in Sotheby's).

- zShops, where thousands of small merchants can do business under the Amazon.com banner.

- Credit cards in a cobranded arrangement with NextCard Inc. (Amazon.com also spent $22.5 million for a warrant that lets it acquire 9.9 percent of the credit-card company.)

Wow! What a list. But, hey, if you're "person of the year," you ought to be able to do all of these things.

Amazon.com used to use the theme "Earth's Biggest Book-

118

store." No longer. They've changed it. The new theme is "Earth's Biggest Selection."

Person of the year Jeff Bezos, CEO of Amazon.com, says, "It's very natural for a customer to wonder, can you really be the best place to buy music, books and electronics? In the physical world, the answer is almost always no. But on the Internet all the physical constraints go away." (A sign of the times: The company recently registered "Amazoneverywhere.net as a Website name.)

All the physical constraints may go away on the Internet, but what about the mental constraints? What about the mind of the prospect. What's an Amazon.com?

If Xerox is copiers, IBM is computers, Cadillac is big cars, and Volkswagen is small cars, then Amazon.com is an Internet bookstore.

If Amazon.com is an Internet bookstore, then how come the site has also been able to successfully sell music CDs? And if they can successfully sell music CDs, why can't they also sell toys and electronics?

Look around your community at big bookstores like Borders or Waldenbooks. Do they sell toys and electronics? No. But they do sell music CDs. Ergo: The customer associates music CDs with bookstores.

"There's no reason for Amazon not to sell other merchandise," said Bill Gates recently. Yes, there is. It's called "perception," and it's a critical attribute of the human mind. Amazon.com means Internet bookstore. Not auctions, gifts, home improvement products, toys, video games, electronics, software, DVDs, or videotapes.

You see Amazon.com thinking all over the physical world. Blockbuster means video rentals. "There's no reason for Blockbuster Video not to sell other merchandise," someone at corporate headquarters probably muttered to themselves a number of years ago. So Blockbuster Music was born.

After years of losses, the company finally faced the music and spun off the division in 1999. The new name: Wherehouse Music.

Boston Chicken meant rotisserie chicken. "There's no reason for Boston Chicken not to sell other food products," figured top management. So the company changed the name of its stores to Boston Market and added turkey, meat loaf, and ham to the menu.

Were you surprised that Boston Chicken recently went bankrupt? Vanity strikes again.

"You'll see more Amazon-like cases in which a company that is strong in one online area expands its product offerings," adds Bill Gates. Sure, you will. Line extension is very popular in corporate America, almost as popular as stock options. Both feed the corporate ego.

What is terribly confusing is the fact that line extension can work . . . in the short term. But almost never in the long term.

This is especially true if you are the first in a new category. When you are the first, when you dominate a new category, you can be successful in the short term taking the line-extension route. You may pay the price later, but you can easily fool yourself into thinking that you are going in the right direction when you broaden your approach.

Take Yahoo!, for example. Incredibly the company's mission statement is "to be all things to all people" (a phrase reportedly repeated as a mantra by many Yahoo! executives).

Starting as a search engine on the Internet, Yahoo! has now expanded its Website to include the following features: auctions, calendars, chat rooms, classifieds, e-mail, games, maps, news, pager services, people searches, personals, radio, shopping, sports, stock quotes, weather reports, and yellow pages.

To further its goal of being all things to all people, Yahoo! has also spent a small fortune on a raft of acquisitions.

- $5 billion for Broadcast.com, a service that delivers audio and video over the Internet.

- $3.7 billion for GeoCities, a home-page service.

- $130 million for Encompass, a technology company that makes software to more easily link consumers to Internet services.

- $80 million for Online Anywhere, a technology that allows the company to deliver information and services to a wide variety of non-PC devices.

Is Yahoo! successful? (Silly question, the company is worth $114 billion.)

Sure, Yahoo! is successful, but the brand had the enormous advantage of being the first search engine on the Internet. As a result, Yahoo! received an inordinate amount of publicity.

Yahoo! became a celebrity brand. In one seventeen-month period, in six thousand different news media, Yahoo! received an astounding forty-five thousand citations, far greater than any other Internet site.

Nothing succeeds like excess. With enough favorable media mentions, Mussolini Merlot might become a popular brand of Italian wine.

But nothing lasts forever. The media will move on to the next hot Internet brand, leaving Yahoo! in the uncomfortable position of having to spend its own money to communicate its identity.

What's a Yahoo!? Not an easy question to answer when you are "all things to all people."

Leaders tend to self-destruct when they blow themselves up. When you try to be everything, you end up being nothing.

Apple started as a personal computer hardware company, then moved into software, operating systems, and personal digital assistants. Apple lost its way, its CEO, and almost its entire existence until Steve Jobs retook the reins and refocused Apple on its core business, easy-to-use and "insanely great" personal computers.

But everybody wants to grow, and you can't blame them. So what should an Internet brand like Amazon.com do? There are five fundamental branding strategies for a leader in any category.

1. Keep your brand focused.

There are more than 5 million dotcom sites registered on the Internet, and you want your site to stand for more than one thing? Amazon.com should stay focused on books and music

CDs. After all, the site accounts for just 4 percent of the $24.6 billion book market in the United States.

2. Increase your share of the market.

The time to think about getting into another business is after you dominate the business you're already in. Until Amazon.com has at least 25 percent of the book market, they should stick to their knitting.

3. Expand your market.

Leaders should figure out how to expand their market, knowing that many of the benefits of a larger market will flow to them. What about book clubs, chat rooms with authors, and other book-building activities, including Amazon-sponsored seminars by famous authors?

4. Go global.

Sure, the Internet is a worldwide information and communications network already, but Amazon.com's share of the book market outside the United States is minuscule. (Currently the company sells only 22 percent of its books overseas, where 95 percent of the world lives.)

Amazon.com should make a major effort to reach customers in the rest of the world. As English becomes the business language of the world, the market for books in English should skyrocket.

Why stop at English? Amazon.com should take its Internet expertise into all the major languages of the world.

Thinking often stops at the border. The most successful companies today treat the world as their oyster.

5. Dominate the category.

For a leading brand, a 25 percent market share should be a conservative goal. With a quarter of the U.S. book market, Amazon.com would rack up sales of $6.6 billion, enough to put the company on the *Fortune* 500 list, ahead of such companies as General Dynamics, General Mills, Ryder Systems, Nordstrom, Owens Corning, Black & Decker, and Hershey Foods.

Nothing works in branding as well as market domination. Coca-Cola in cola, Hertz in car rentals, Budweiser in beer, Goodyear in tires, Microsoft in personal computer operating systems, Intel in microprocessors, Cisco in routers, Oracle in database software, Intuit in personal finance software.

Amazon.com has a once-in-a-lifetime opportunity to dominate the book business on a worldwide scale. Why throw away this opportunity in order to chase a dozen other markets, none of which they are likely to dominate?

Still, when the vanity bug bites you, it's hard to resist. "We can get into these other markets. We have the products, we have the people, we have the systems, we have the momentum, and we have the esprit de corps. Why not?"

Why not? You may have everything going for you, including the products, the people, and the systems, but you lack one thing. You lack the perception.

The issue in branding, Internet or otherwise, always boils down to the same thing: product versus perception.

Many managers believe it's only necessary to deliver a better product or service to win. But brands like Coca-Cola, Hertz, Budweiser, and Goodyear are strong not because they have the best product or service (although they might have) but because they are market leaders that dominate their categories.

Which scenario seems more likely, A or B?

Scenario A: The company creates a better product or service and consequently achieves market leadership.

Scenario B: The company achieves market leadership (usually by being first in a new category) and then subsequently achieves the perception of having the better product or service.

Logic suggests Scenario A, but history is overwhelmingly on the side of Scenario B. Leadership first, perception second.

AltaVista bills itself as "the most powerful and useful guide to the Net." We have no reason to doubt their claim. But is this enough to enable AltaVista to wrestle the portal leadership away from Yahoo!? Not in our opinion.

125

Leadership first, perception second. To try to reverse this sequence is almost impossible.

What if you do everything right? What if you are the first in a new category and subsequently go on to dominate that category domestically? Then you should try to expand the market in the U.S. at the same time that you take your brand to the global market.

Coca-Cola did all of these things. But what's next? Are there no second acts in branding history?

Most assuredly there are. A company can do two things at once (keep a narrow focus and expand its business) by the simple strategy of launching a second, or even a third and fourth, brand.

- Coca-Cola owns Coca-Cola, the leading cola, and Sprite, the leading lemon-lime soda.

- Anheuser-Busch owns Budweiser, the leading regular beer; Michelob, the leading premium beer; and Busch, the leading low-price beer.

- Darden Restaurants owns Olive Garden, the leading Italian restaurant chain, and Red Lobster, the leading seafood restaurant chain. (Darden is the world's largest casual dining company.)

- Toyota also owns Lexus.

- Black & Decker also owns DeWalt.

- Levi Strauss owns both Levi's and Dockers.

- The Gap also owns Banana Republic and Old Navy.

America Online is using the same multiple-brand strategy on the Internet. AOL is its premium brand for which subscribers pay $21.95 a month. The service includes nineteen separate topic channels, fifteen thousand chat rooms, and ICQ, a popular instant messaging capability. CompuServe is the company's value brand. For the same monthly access charge, CompuServe offers cash rebates to new subscribers who agree to purchase certain computers.

Instead of launching second brands, however, most companies take the vanity route instead. "What's wrong with our name? We're famous. Why do we need a second brand? We can use our own name on that line extension."

Some companies that practice line extension seem to be successful, at least in the short term. Microsoft is a good example.

After dominating the personal computer operating system business, Microsoft has gone into a raft of different businesses, all under the Microsoft name. "If Microsoft can do it, why can't we?" is a constant refrain of our consulting clients.

Our answer: You're not Microsoft. When you have more than 90 percent of a market, when you are worth more than half a trillion dollars on the stock market, you are extremely powerful. You can do almost anything and still appear to be successful.

Leadership changes the rules of the game. Try telling your spouse, "If Bill Clinton can do it, why can't I?"

Most CEOs are not Bill Clinton either. They are not the leader of the most powerful country in the world. They have to follow ordinary rules.

Leaders, especially dominant leaders like Microsoft, can break all the laws and still stay on top . . . for now.

Look again at Yahoo!, a company that is following the Microsoft game plan. CEO Timothy Koogle says: "In online commerce and shopping you can expect to see us extend aggressively by broadening and deepening the range of consumer buying, transaction, and fulfillment services we provide across all major categories."

(Don't be too critical of Yahoo!'s behavior. You only live once. Being young and rich and foolish is a lot more fun than being old and wise.)

Many sites are going in the same direction, but without Yahoo!'s powerful brand-name recognition. They include Buy.com, Shopping.com, Shopnow.com, and a host of other copycat sites. "Anything you want to buy, we can get it for you at a discount."

What does a site like BuyItNow.com sell? Jewelry, consumer electronics, toys, kitchen equipment, home decorating products, sporting goods, tools, pet supplies, garden supplies, gifts, luxury items. "You name it, we've got it."

Snap.com goes one step further. Not only can you buy everything by visiting the Snap site, but you can buy it from any store. "Any product. Any store. Any time. Snap shopping" is the theme. Vanity is working overtime at Snap.com.

When Internet fever cools down, when the Internet is just one of the places you can go to buy things, those generic sites that sell everything to everybody are unlikely to be with us. Yahoo!, on the other hand, is in no danger because it has a powerful, dominant position in the portal category. As does Amazon.com in the books and music category.

A question remains for leader brands like Yahoo! and Amazon.com. Would these companies have been better off with a multiple-brand strategy rather than a line-extension strategy?

We think so. But it is getting harder and harder to find leaders that want to introduce second brands.

Their vanity leads them astray.

10

The Law of Divergence

Everyone talks about convergence,
while just the opposite is happening.

Whenever a new medium hits town, the cry goes up, "Convergence, convergence. What is this new medium going to converge with?"

When television hit town, there were stories everywhere about the convergence of TV with magazines and newspapers. You weren't going to get your magazines in the mail anymore. When you wanted an issue, you would hit the button on your TV set and the issue would be printed out in your living room. (We don't make these things up. We just report the facts.)

When the Internet arrived, the same type of stories appeared. Now you can surf the Net while you watch TV. (Microsoft's WebTV is the leading supplier of the service.)

Many companies have tried to combine a television set with a personal computer, with a notable lack of success—Apple, Gateway, and others.

Convergence has become an obsession at Microsoft. "Has William H. Gates become the Captain Ahab of the information age?" asked the *New York Times* recently. "Mr. Gates' white

whale remains an elusive digital set-top cable box that his company, the Microsoft Corporation, is hoping will re-create the
personal computer industry by blending the PC, the Internet
and the television set into a leviathan living-room entertainment and information machine."

The PC, the Internet, and the television set will combine? It
will never happen. Technologies don't converge. They diverge.

Many Internet branders are falling into the convergence
trap. They look for ways to blend the real world with the
Internet world. Their ingenuity knows no bounds.

- Newspapers and magazines on the Internet.

- Radio and television on the Internet.

- Internet service on your telephone or from your PalmPilot.

- Facsimile and telephone service from your computer or
  television set.

The media have been fanning the convergence fire for a long
time. According to a 1993 article in the *Wall Street Journal*:

Shock is a common feeling these days among leaders of five
of the world's biggest industries: computing, communications, consumer electronics, entertainment and publishing.
Under a common technological lash—the increasing ability
to cheaply convey huge chunks of video, sound, graphics
and text in digital form—they are transforming and con-
verging.

The *New York Times* put it this way:

Digital convergence is not a futuristic prospect or a choice to be made among other choices; it is an onrushing train. The digitalization of all forms of information (including the transmission of sensations) has proven itself to be accurate, economical, ecologically wise, universally applicable, easy to use, and fast as light.

Fortune was just as enthusiastic:

Convergence will be the buzzword for the rest of the decade. This isn't just about cable and telephone hopping into bed together. It's about the cultures and corporations of major industries—telecommunications (including the long-distance companies), cable, computers, entertainment, consumer electronics, publishing, and even retailing—combining into one mega-industry that will provide information, entertainment, goods, and services to your home and office.

The media are putting their money where their mouths are. The *Wall Street Journal* publishes a magazine called *Convergence*. *Forbes* recently published a special issue entitled "The Great Convergence." *Business Week* runs an annual conference entitled "The Global Convergence Summit."

With the media running off at the mouth about the convergence concept, is it any wonder that many corporations were all too eager to jump on the bandwagon? When asked by

Fortune magazine what unique opportunities Compaq was looking at, the new CEO, Michael Capellas, said: "You'll start to see devices converge. Who in the world doesn't want to have their PalmPilot, their telephone, and their CD player all wrapped into one so they don't have to carry three things on their belt?"

It will never happen. Technologies don't converge. They diverge. Yet the hype marches on.

According to one famous futurist, "Someday in the near future I'll be watching *Ally McBeal*. I like the outfit she's wearing. So I put my hand on the TV screen and she'll interrupt the program and say, 'Faith, do you like what I'm wearing?' 'Yeah,' I'll say. 'I like your suit.' And she'll say, 'Here are the colors it comes in.' I'll tell Ally that I'll take just navy or black, maybe both. And she'll say, 'No you won't, Faith. You've already got too many navy and black outfits in your closet right now. I think you should try red this time.' And I'll say okay, and the next day the red suit is delivered, in my size, to my home."

When asked how soon this would happen, the famous futurist replied, "Within the next five years."

Don't hold your breath. Ally McBeal will be lucky if her TV show is still on in five years, never mind her personal shopping advice service.

While television sets and telephones are supposedly becoming computers, computers are supposedly becoming appliances that can receive television and radio programming as well as telephone calls.

Broadcast.com, for example, offers live broadcasts of more

than thirty television stations and 370 radio stations. All available on your computer through the magic of the Internet. Meanwhile, rival Real Networks has put together more than 1,100 live stations on their lineup. Competitor InterVU has put together a network focused on business services.

Will people watch television programming on their computers? Sure, some people will, but most television viewing is likely to continue to be done on TV sets.

The truth is, technologies divide. They don't converge. A quick look at history validates the division theory.

- Radio used to be just radio. Today we have AM radio and FM radio. We also have portable radios, car radios, headset radios, clock radios, cable radio, and satellite radio. Radio didn't combine with another medium. It divided.

- Television used to be just television. Today we have broadcast TV, cable TV, satellite TV, pay-per-view TV. Television didn't combine with another medium. It divided.

- The telephone used to be just the telephone. Today we have regular telephones, cordless telephones, car phones, mobile phones, and satellite phones. Also analog and digital phones. The telephone didn't combine with another communications technology. It divided.

- The computer used to be just a computer. Today we have mainframe computers, midrange computers, minicomputers, network computers, personal computers, notebook computers, and palm computers. The computer didn't combine with another technology. It divided.

135

People often confuse what's possible with what's practical. After Neil Armstrong and Buzz Aldrin walked on the moon in 1969, the media were filled with stories about future colonists in space. Where they would live. What they would eat. How they would work.

(The moon is a great place to visit, but how many people would want to live there?)

What's possible won't happen just because it's possible. It also has to be practical. Computers and television would seem like a natural, but Apple, Toshiba, Gateway, and others have launched combination products that failed.

Recently Philips went one step further. In addition to a computer and a television tuner, the Philips DVX8000 features an FM/AM radio and a CD/DVD player. What more could you want?

Simplicity, ease of use, reliability, light weight, protection against early obsolescence, and low cost, for example.

Instead of accessing the Internet from your home television set, it is much more likely that you will someday have an Internet appliance. An electronic machine devoted to Internet connections only. (Divergence at work.)

Actually there are a number of such products on the market. For $199, you can get the i-opener from Netpliance, a device that does just Web browsing and e-mail. If you're interested in e-mail only, you can order the e-Mail PostBox from VTech Industries and save $100. (The BlackBerry is another divergence device that has quite a few enthusiastic users.)

Why are divergence products generally winners and convergence products generally losers? One reason is that convergence products are always a compromise. The Intel micro-processor inside the Philips DVX8000 should be good for three years or so. The home-theater half of the machine should last twenty years.

Before televisions combine with computers, you would think TV sets would combine with videocassette recorders. You can buy combination TV/VCRs, of course, but most people don't. Recently we visited a consumer electronics store that had a wall full of such products.

"How are sales of your combination television/VCRs?" we asked the clerk. "Infinitesimal," he replied.

Nor are many combination washer/dryers sold. Or microwave/stoves. Or telephone/telephone answering machines. Or copier/printer/fax machines.

The one glimmer of hope for the convergence concept is the clock radio. Enthusiasts are fond of citing the clock radio as a brilliant example of the power of convergence thinking. But in some ways, a clock radio is not a dual function device at all. Rather, it's a single-function music alarm clock, a way of getting you out of bed in the morning without the shock of an earth-shattering noise. Not many people use their clock radios as a way to play the radio.

Other than the clock radio, the history of convergence products has been rather dismal. After World War II, the two biggest industries in America were the automotive industry and the airplane industry. Sure enough, pundits thought that the car was going to converge with the airplane.

In 1945, Ted Hall introduced his Flying Car, which was received by a wildly enthusiastic public. Roads soon would become obsolete, traffic jams a thing of the past. You could go anywhere, anytime, with complete freedom of movement. Every major aircraft manufacturer in America hoped to cash in on Hall's invention. The lucky buyer was Convair.

In July of 1946, Convair introduced Hall's flight of fancy as the Convair Model 118 ConvAirCar. Company management confidently predicted minimum sales of 160,000 units a year. The price was $1,500 plus an extra charge for the wings, which would also be available for rental at any airport.

In spite of the hype, only two ConvAirCars were ever built. Both are now said to rest in a warehouse in El Cajon, California.

Three years later, Moulton Taylor introduced the Aerocar, a sporty runabout with detachable wings and tail. The Aerocar received a tremendous amount of publicity at the time. The Ford Motor Company considered mass-producing it. But Taylor's Aerocar met with the same predictable fate as Hall's Flying Car.

It's divergence that almost always triumphs, not convergence. Today we have many types of airplanes (jet planes, prop planes, helicopters) and many types of automobiles (sedans, convertibles, station wagons, sport utility vehicles), but almost no flying cars.

Would-be convergenists should also study the combination automobile/boat introduced with great fanfare by Amphicar, a German company. Like all convergence products, the Amphicar performed neither function very well. "Drives like a boat, floats like a car," was the buyers' verdict.

Bad ideas never really die. Paul Moller has spent thirty-five years developing the Skycar, a personal flying machine that is as easy to use as a car. Today, $50 million, forty-three patents, and three wives later, his dream is ready for liftoff.

Don't laugh. What will look foolish several decades from now is often taken seriously today. As recently as June 24, 1999, the *Wall Street Journal* ran a major article on Moller's sky dream on the front page of its Marketplace section.

What motivates Moller also motivates Microsoft. The company is pouring millions of dollars into WebTV, a major effort to turn America's 100 million television-owning households into Internet explorers.

Sure, WebTV is closing in on 1 percent of the market, but does any convergence product have much of a future? (Professor Moller has taken seventy-two orders, with a $5,000 deposit, for the Skycar.)

There's a lot of evidence that mixing "interactivity," an Internet attribute, with the "passivity" of the television experience just isn't going to work. Time Warner introduced the Full Service Network, the first digital interactive TV network, in Orlando, Florida, in 1994 and shut it down two years later.

A company called ACTV was founded in 1989 to bring interactive TV to the public. On average the company has lost $7 million a year for the past decade. Finally, ACTV is rolling out its first product in partnership with Fox Sports. For $10 a month, Fox fans will be able to use their remote control to click on to different camera angles, pull up stats, or cut to instant replays at any time during the game.

Will the average couch potato want to put down his Bud Light long enough to change the camera angle? We don't think so. At least not when the home team is third down and goal to go.

TV directors get paid big bucks to do that for us. Why would the average viewer want to do it for nothing?

Not only that. Spending the time figuring out the best camera angle will cause the watcher to miss the play. Not to mention the frustrations of the other people in the room who do not have the remote control in their hands.

Technology tends to triumph over logic. "If you build it, they will come." Bill Gates, the manager of the high technology team, is getting his players involved in convergence in a big way. In addition to his WebTV investment, Gates has put $5 billion of Microsoft's money into AT&T to help the company purchase a cable TV operation. In return, AT&T has agreed to license a minimum of five million copies of Microsoft's Windows CE operating system.

The two companies are hoping that a General Instrument set-top box, the DTC-5000, will be the entry point for all the digital information flowing into the home. In addition to five hundred channels of interactive cable, the DTC-5000 will handle telephone service, video on demand, stereo audio, video games, and Internet access. An information-age Cuisinart is what some pundits are calling the box.

The Skycar, the Amphicar, the set-top box. Billions of dollars have been wasted chasing the convergence delusion. But why do we make such a federal case out of the convergence follies?

Because brands cannot be built with convergence thinking. Unless you can clearly see the fallacy behind the convergence concept, you are unlikely to build a successful Internet brand. Most Internet ideas, most Internet brands, most Internet companies are based on convergence concepts. That's why most Internet brands will fail.

- What if you could find home selection, home buying, home selling, and home mortgages at one easy-to-use Website? (Homeadvisor.com)

- What if you could use your computer to listen to radio broadcasts? All you need are speakers or headphones and audio software. (Spinner.com, Imagineradio.com, Netradio.com)

- What if you could use your computer to watch television broadcasts? (WinTV, AT1 Technologies)

- What if you could use your mobile phone to surf the Web, send and receive e-mail, and transfer data to a PC? (NeoPoint, Nextel, Sprint PCS)

- What if you could use your computer to listen to music? (MP3.com)

"People used to have to go to three or four different places to get something done" is the premise of many of our consulting clients. "With our new Website, they'll be able to do one-stop shopping." (Whoops. Another client that needs to get the convergence speech.)

We get our hair cut and our clothes dry-cleaned at two different places, but we're quite sure that doesn't spell "opportunity" for some would-be entrepreneur. (We used to get our hair cut and our nails done at one place. Now we go to two different places. That's divergence in action.)

Why do things divide? Divergence is consistent with the laws of nature, convergence is not.

In physics, for instance, the law of entropy says the degree of disorder in a closed system always increases. By contrast, a pattern of convergence would make things more orderly.

In biology, the law of evolution holds that new species are created by the division of a single species. Convergence, instead, suggests that the combining of two species will yield a new one.

Invariably in nature you see things divide and not converge. We have hundreds of varieties of dogs and hundreds of varieties of cats, but very few dogcats, or chickenducks, or horsecows.

A company is going against the laws of nature when it tries to build an Internet brand on the convergence concept. "Are you getting three different kinds of electronic messages— voice-mail, e-mail, and fax? Fine, we can fix that for you."

These new all-in-one services are called "unified messaging sites." Instead of having to dial into your voice-mail, open your e-mail, or check your fax machine, you just go to the sponsor's Web page and get all your messages (Messagesclick.com, Onebox.com, Telebot.com, MReach.com).

What's wrong with a unified messaging service? Nothing, except it drives like a boat and floats like a car.

11

The Law of Transformation

*The Internet revolution will transform
all aspects of our lives.*

I n business there is never only one way to do anything.

- Some people prefer to shop in specialty stores, some people in department stores.

- Some people prefer to shop in supermarkets, some in neighborhood stores.

- Some people love shopping malls, some don't.

- Some people love to buy from catalogs, some don't.

- Some people go to Wal-Mart because the prices are low. Some people go to Neiman-Marcus because the prices are high.

- Some people will turn to the Internet for much of their shopping, information, and communication needs. Some people won't.

- Some products and services will be sold or distributed primarily over the Internet. Some products and services won't.

If your product or service is in the latter category, you might think that you have nothing to gain from the Net. But, in our opinion, you would be wrong.

The Internet will affect your business whether you jump on the Web or not. What changes will the Internet bring to your business and your life? The future is always fuzzy, but here are some predictions.

1. Paper directories are doomed.

You won't be surprised to learn that the *Encyclopaedia Britannica,* published since 1768, will no longer be available in a paper version. From now on the encyclopedia will only be available online or on CD-ROM.

The companies that publish "yellow pages" telephone directories ought to be concerned. The fingers that used to go walking though those directories are now rapidly moving to the keyboard.

"Information at your fingertips," said Microsoft in its early advertising efforts. And it's true. The plumber, the electrician, the veterinarian, the auto dealer can be more quickly found and evaluated on an electronic directory than on a paper one.

What will happen to the $12 billion that companies spend

annually on yellow pages advertising? Good question. We'd be concerned if we made our living publishing or selling space in a paper directory.

Paper directories are doomed because of the interactivity of the Internet. The user can manipulate a single computer database in literally thousands of ways.

Furthermore, the database can be updated daily, even hourly. A typical "yellow pages" directory comes out once a year and is out-of-date the day it lands on your doorstep.

Even some great paper institutions are going to have trouble competing in the future. The 116-year-old full *Oxford English Dictionary* could cease to exist after it goes online on a subscription basis. The dictionary, which runs to twenty volumes and costs $2,900, is a dinosaur in the Internet age.

2. Paper catalogs face an uncertain future.

Mailboxes across the county are stuffed with countless catalogs every day. According to one estimate, 17.6 billion catalogs were mailed in the U.S. last year. That's sixty-four catalogs for every man, woman, and child.

That may change. Catalogs of all types will find themselves under severe electronic competition. There are a number of reasons why a Web catalog is superior to a paper one.

An electronic catalog can be interactive. You can sort by types, sizes, colors, prices, weights, and so on. Think

Amazon.com, for example. You can sort by author, by title, by subject, by category. In contrast, a paper catalog of books is so impractical that few are printed and distributed, except for narrow selections.

Furthermore, an electronic catalog is much less expensive to distribute. Once the material is composed in an electronic format, the cost of distribution is essentially zero. Manufacturing a paper catalog, however, can be costly. Just to print those 17.6 billion mail-order missiles requires 3.35 million tons of paper.

So what do you do if you're L.L. Bean? Good question.

Sales have been essentially flat at L.L. Bean for the last few years. That puts pressure on the bottom line because the company prints and mails catalogs thirty times a year. And printing and mailing costs continue to rise.

So L.L. Bean opens up a Website to sell the same merchandise found in the catalog. Is this a good idea or not?

Yes and no. In general, when you broaden the scope of a brand, you weaken the brand. In the long run, multiple distribution channels substantially increase costs and do not do much to increase sales.

A fully functioning Website with computer hardware and service people backed by a programming staff is not an inexpensive proposition.

To get the company moving again, L.L. Bean is opening a chain of retail stores, in addition to its nine factory outlet stores. Outlets are one thing, they help you get rid of leftovers. When you open retail stores, however, you are competing directly with yourself, never a good idea.

A better solution for L.L. Bean and other catalog companies is to shift the entire operation to the Web. Don't try to maintain two expensive distribution channels for a brand whose market is limited.

You can't do this overnight. You need transition time. We would gradually reduce the number of catalogs mailed and shift some of the savings into publicity and advertising programs for the Website. You need a way to drive prospects to your site.

One of the major advantages of ordering products from a computer rather than from a catalog is the interactivity of the Website. You know instantly whether or not the product is in stock in the color and/or size you want.

(This, of course, is only a theoretical advantage. Many sites have yet to integrate their warehousing operations with their order-entry systems.)

When you call to order from a catalog, inevitably at least one of the items you want is out of stock or back-ordered.

Should every catalog company shift to the Web? Of course not. There is never only one way to do anything. For certain products in certain categories, the better strategy might be to remain a catalog-only company. As catalog mailings taper off, the remaining companies in the field will find that their individual catalogs have become more productive.

3. The elaborate full-color brochure will become exceedingly rare.

Many companies will rethink their use of expensive brochures, which are virtually out-of-date the day they come off the press. It's a lot more efficient to let a prospect stroll through your Website to look at the same information.

If something catches the prospect's eye, they can always print out the page using one of the many inexpensive color printers now on the market.

One way to promote a seminar, for example, is to send out inexpensive mass mailings (postcards maybe) and then invite prospects to get all the details on your Website.

Annual reports of corporations are another category of printed brochure that is headed for extinction. It may take a while, however, for the Securities and Exchange Commission to change the regulations that govern their use.

4. Classified advertising will shift to the Web.

A big chunk of newspapers' revenues comes from their classifieds. This is a category that will come under immense pressure from the Web. Houses, apartments, job listings, in particular.

Take the help-wanted category, for example. The first Website to tackle this category was Monster.com, which today leads the Web in online job listings. (Create a new category you can be first in is the classic marketing strategy for potential leaders, whether on the Web or in the physical world.)

Currently the site does $100 million in revenues by charging companies for job listings and access to its 1.5 million résumés. More than seven million people visit the site each month, eyeing 227,000 jobs. Monster.com even turns a profit.

Long term, the Internet will seriously erode a major source of local newspaper revenues. What should the *Daily Bugle* do about this?

In retrospect the answer is easy. Open a job-listing Website before Monster.com came on the scene. Who knows more about the help-wanted market than the newspaper industry? The companies that spend money today with Monster.com have been their customers for years.

That's the way it often is. The people who know the most about a given market or industry are often the least likely to see the change coming. The motto of many major corporations is: "Hear no change. See no change. Speak no change."

5. The postal service won't be delivering as much mail.

The words "Letter Carrier" used to be prominently displayed on postal service uniforms. No more. Today the average letter carrier doesn't carry very many letters. That business has gone electronic, either to phone, facsimile, or e-mail.

In a recent year, more than four trillion e-mail messages were sent, more than forty times the 99.7 billion pieces of first-class mail delivered by the postal service.

The largest segment of first-class mail today is bills, invoices, and financial statements. The sending and paying of bills alone accounts for $17 billion, or almost 30 percent of the postal service's revenue. That segment is going to be especially vulnerable to the Internet.

Look at what happens when a company bills a customer for a product or service the customer has ordered—for example, a telephone company's monthly phone bill.

The telephone company's mainframe computer prints out an invoice, which is stuffed into an envelope, and first-class postage is applied. After the postal service delivers the bill, the customer writes a check, puts it in the return envelope, and adds a first-class postage stamp. After the postal service delivers the envelope, the phone company opens the envelope and deposits the check in its bank account. (So far the round-trip postage alone has cost sixty-six cents, minus the postal service's small discount for presorted first-class mail.)

What happens next is the interesting part. The bank's computers make an upward adjustment in the amount of money in the phone company's account and a downward adjustment in the amount of money in the customer's account. (This, of course, is the case when both the seller and buyer use the same bank. Otherwise more transactions between banks are necessary.)

All that paperwork, all that postage, all that human effort

just to shift a number in a computer from Column A to Column B.

People forget that money, for the most part, is not steel engravings printed on paper. It's not even gold in a vault. Money is electronic bits of information stored on computers around the world. To shift money from one account to another, you shift the bits.

The sending and paying of bills online is an idea whose time has come. We foresee a rapid rise in electronic banking and a rapid decline in the number of pieces of first-class mail sent and received.

If you think that can't happen soon, look at the phenomenal rise in e-mail, which is increasing at the rate of almost 50 percent a year. Can e-banking be far behind?

According to a recent report issued by the General Accounting Office, "The Postal Service may be nearing the end of an era."

6. Financial services of all types will shift to the Web.

Because money is nothing more than bits on a computer, the entire financial services industry is headed for the Internet.

It just makes sense to have your bank account in your bedroom or office, where you can check invoices, pay bills, shift funds, and borrow money, all by manipulating bits on a bank's computer.

The computer revolutionized the banking industry once before with the introduction of the automated teller machine. What the ATM has started, the computer (in combination with the Internet) will finish. There's no reason why banking and most financial transactions, including insurance and stock brokerage, should not be handled on the Internet.

Shifting financial transactions to the Internet can result in substantial savings. It costs, on average, $4.20 for a bank teller to handle a customer transaction that an ATM machine can handle for $1.10. That same transaction on the Internet might cost just 10 cents.

That's the tip of the financial iceberg. The real savings will come from invoicing and bill paying. About seventy billion checks are issued in the United States every year. (That's 260 checks for every person.) Much of this paper blizzard can be easily moved to the Net, saving money and improving the record keeping of both businesses and individuals.

One concern, of course, is the inability of your computer to deal out real money the way an ATM machine does. But this might not turn out to be much of a problem. Paper money is declining in importance as more people shift to credit, debit, and check cards for the bulk of their purchases.

You can spend a week on the road (and we have) without using paper money, with the exception of small bills for tips, taxis, and newspapers. And even taxicab companies are starting to take credit cards. It will probably be a while before bellmen at hotels or porters at airports swipe credit cards. (With credit cards, they would have to declare their tip income on their tax returns.)

7. The parcel delivery business will soar.

The Internet will greatly stimulate business for all of the parcel delivery companies. UPS (United Parcel Service) might want to change its name to IPS (Internet Parcel Service).

As a result of the increases in volume, you can expect delivery prices to hold steady or even decline.

The weak link in the system is the front door of the customer. With so many DINK (double income, no kids) families in the country, many customers will not be home when the delivery person arrives.

Some companies are already working on this problem. Smartbox, for example, is a locked, reinforced box that comes in various sizes and sits outside your home. To allow access to all delivery services, the device will be wired to the Internet. When the box owner makes an online purchase, special software will create and transmit a code for each order. A delivery driver can punch in the code on a keypad to unlock the box and make the delivery.

8. Internet retailing will become a price game.

Will most products be bought in cyberspace? Probably not. But the Internet will drastically change the focus of most retailers.

Some retailers are worried. Home Depot, which is on the

verge of selling its own products over the Internet, is rapping the knuckles of suppliers that have similar dreams. The retailer recently sent a letter to all of its vendors telling them to think twice before selling their tools and equipment directly to consumers though their Websites.

"We think it is shortsighted for vendors to ignore the added value that our retail stores contribute to the sales of their products," stated the Home Depot letter.

How will the Internet change retailing in the future? To understand the revolution to come, it might be helpful to take a look at the history of retailing. Fifty years ago, the largest and most successful retailer in the world was Sears, Roebuck & Co.

What was Sears known for? It wasn't a single product category, since Sears sold everything. If Volvo stands for "safety," BMW stands for "driving," and Nordstrom stands for "service," we think you would find that Sears, Roebuck & Co. stood for "trust." (The company has a lot of research to show that this perception was true.)

Customers trusted Sears to sell them good products at reasonable prices.

Is this any less true today? No. Then what changed? It wasn't Sears. They still sell good products at reasonable prices: Kenmore refrigerators, DieHard batteries, Craftsman tools, and other Sears brands.

What changed is the rise of national brands. Since the glory days of Sears, Roebuck, the country has experienced a tremendous increase in the number of well-known, well-regarded national brands. To name a few: Maytag, Black &

Decker, Goodyear, KitchenAid, Cuisinart, Sony, Nintendo, Ralph Lauren, Levi's.

(Sears acknowledged the power of national brands, as opposed to the retailer's house brands, by creating its "Brand Central" concept a number of years ago.)

With the rise of national brands, the nature of retailing changed. The "trust" was built into the brand name. The only thing the retailer supplied was the "product" at a certain "price."

People trust Sears, but they buy from Wal-Mart. The brands are exactly the same, but the prices at Wal-Mart are lower. "We sell for less," as their advertisements say.

National brands allow prospects to compare retail prices in many different categories. Retailing has become a price game. And Wal-Mart, not Sears, has become the world's largest retailer.

Price has become the main driver of the retail industry. Pick up any newspaper in the country and look at the retail ads. What do you find? It's what the industry calls "item and price" advertising. Just a listing of the brand name, the product category, the size, and the price.

"Star-Kist tuna, 6 oz. can, 89¢."

Walk down any retail street in America and look at the store windows. What do you see? "Sale" signs. We walked down a retail street recently and counted twelve stores in a row with a sale sign in their windows. It wasn't until we reached the thirteenth store that we found one without a sale sign.

The price game causes many problems for manufacturers. Retailers often demand exclusivity in their territories so they can advertise "the lowest price in town." Manufacturers go along with these demands by producing a bewildering variety of models, colors, and sizes. (Mattress and bedding makers are notorious in this respect.)

Wal-Mart and the mass merchandisers are known for demanding special sizes so they can get a bigger discount and customers can't as easily compare prices with the same products at other retail stores. Then there are special purchases, end-of-product runs, obsolete products, manufacturers' seconds, and a host of other strategies for generating low prices on the retail floor. There are also gray-market products brought in from other countries. (Which is why you might see a Mach 3 razor in Costco with the package printed in French.)

The Internet will change the nature of retailing by pulling the plug on many of these "price" promotions. If all the customer really wants is the absolute lowest price, then the place to shop is the Net.

Instead of reading a lot of different ads or driving from store to store, a prospect can sit down at a keyboard and quickly compare prices on a similar item from a large number of sources.

Furthermore, you can also use an "agent" to help you. Agent companies like ClickTheButton, DealPilot, and RUSure have developed software that will scan various shopping sites for price and delivery data, then sort the information (most often by price).

DealTime.com, for example, advertises that it helps you find "exactly what you want, at the price you want, wherever you want." BookPricer.com will help you find "the lowest price for any book in under 30 seconds."

Speaking of books, Amazon.com is discounting *New York Times* bestsellers by 50 percent. Booksamillion.com knocks 55 percent off their top ten bestsellers. (Some publishers don't give their own authors that big a discount. We should know.)

Then there's Buy.com with the tag line, "The lowest prices on Earth." The company is ruthlessly committed to being the price leader, even if this means losing money on every sale. Its technology searches competitors' sites to make sure Buy.com has the lowest prices on the Web. Recently the Palm III Organizer sold for $249 on Buy.com, $330 at CompUSA, and $369 at the manufacturer's own Website.

Buy.com is on track to break Compaq's first-year sales record of $111 million, making it the fastest-growing company in U.S. history. (Their next job is to figure out how to make money.)

And look at the market for low-end personal computers. On the Web, the most common price is "free," with the seller making it up with advertising exposure or a long-term contract for Internet service.

CompUSA, the only physical retailer devoted mainly to personal computers, is closing 14 of its 211 superstores. The Good Guys, which operates eighty consumer electronics stores in the West, announced that it was leaving the PC business altogether.

Bear with us. Physical retailing has nothing to fear from the Internet. But it has to change its current emphasis on low price. It has to find a new focus.

9. Outernet retailing will become a service game.

Just as the rise of national brands put pressure on Sears to change its strategy, the rise of the Internet will put pressure on retailers to change their strategies too.

What retail strategies will work in the shadow of the Internet? We believe the successful retailer of the future will need to play a service game, not a price game. What you might call the Nordstrom approach. (There's no way a physical retailer can compete with an Internet retailer on price.)

The successful outernet retailer of the future will have to emphasize the twin aspects of the physical experience: Touch and Time, or what we have been calling "T 'n' T."

The Touch aspect of the T 'n' T strategy involves the ability of the prospect to hold, feel, taste, smell, handle, and try the product, not just see and read about it. (After all, you can see the product in full color on the Internet.)

Many retailers will have to make their stores a lot more "touch" friendly. Too many products are locked in glass cabinets or entombed in packaging that greatly discourages handling.

In this connection, Saturn's success in creating a more customer-friendly environment is a good pattern for many traditional retailers to adopt.

The Sharper Image also places a high value on the touch aspect of its stores. Customers are encouraged to touch and try the variety of electronic devices in the store.

The Sephora cosmetic chain is another example of the

future of retailing. With its attractive environment, helpful staff, and complete lines, Sephora provides everything a cosmetic buyer might want—except low prices. If you want the absolute lowest cosmetic price, you'll have to go to the Net.

Motion picture exhibitors have gone through this same process as they have upgraded their facilities to compete with HBO, Showtime, and free movies on television. Now you will find smaller theaters, larger, more comfortable seats, multiplex screens. Even the popcorn is getting better.

Price isn't everything. You can drink beer cheaper at home, but every night the bars in our neighborhood are filled with twentysomethings spending a bundle on Bud Light.

The Time aspect of the T 'n' T strategy seems obvious. Unlike on the Net, you save time when you buy from a physical retailer because you don't have to wait for FedEx or UPS to deliver your purchase.

Yet, the time half of an effective T 'n' T strategy is more subtle than that. In theory you don't wait for your purchases when you buy at retail. But in practice the prospect is often frustrated because the store is out of stock. "Come back next week when our new shipment will be in."

The customer of the future will not tolerate a physical retailer with frequent out-of-stock problems. Many of these problems, of course, stem from the retailer's emphasis on low price, which leads to special deals and special purchases. Abandoning a low-price strategy means that a retailer can concentrate on keeping its inventory up-to-date and complete.

Not counting supermarkets, convenience stores, and similar establishments, roughly half the prospects walk out of a general retail store without buying anything. The major reason is that the store didn't have in stock what the customer wanted.

Most business will probably not be conducted over the Web. But the Internet revolution will force every business to adjust its strategy. From a price game to a service game. T 'n' T, if you will.

10. Internet search engines will decline in importance.

Search engines like Yahoo! are busy adding functions when they should be battening down the hatches for the rough water ahead. Search engines (or portals) are going to be less important in the future than they were in the past.

Think of it this way. People get to know the Internet brands they want to do business with. When they do, they will go straight to the site instead of making a detour through a search engine. If we want to buy a book, we go to Amazon.com. We don't go to Yahoo! to find out who on the Net sells books.

This view of the future is consistent with one's own personal experience in the real world. Let's say you move to a new community. You might pick up the yellow pages (paper search engine) every time you go out shopping. After you become familiar with the stores in your new community, you begin to make most of your trips without consulting the yellow pages first.

Yahoo! is the welcome wagon on the Internet. Great for the new arrival, but less important for the experienced Internet user.

11. The Internet will change many aspects of the telephone industry.

In many ways, the Internet and the telephone are similar. Both are information and communications media, but the percentages are different.

If the Internet is 80 percent information and 20 percent communications, the telephone is the opposite. Twenty percent information and 80 percent communications.

The information segment of the telephone medium is a large business in itself even though it accounts for only 20 percent or so of all phone calls. The visible symbol of this information segment, of course, is the yellow pages. "Let your fingers do the walking."

That will change. The Internet will become a direct competitor to the telephone. (Fortunately for the phone companies, most people will continue to use phone lines to connect to the Internet.)

On the communications side, e-mail will replace many phone and fax calls. On the information side, the Net will become an electronic yellow pages.

What television did to radio, the Internet will do to the telephone. TV virtually wiped out entertainment on radio. The Internet will do the same for information on the telephone. Forget 777-FILM and the ten minutes it takes to get playing times for your favorite movie.

For many people the change couldn't come too soon. How many hours have you spent punching in numbers trying to reach someone in Corporate America to help you? The automated call routing systems used by most national companies are a disgrace.

First they answer your call with a variety of options. After punching in an endless series of numbers, you get the following message: "All of our representatives are currently helping other customers, the next available agent will be with you shortly."

By removing the human interface, the Internet promises to greatly speed up the information functions formerly handled on the phone. Airline reservations, movie tickets, reservations for rock concerts and sporting events, restaurant hours and reservations are just some of the information-related transactions that will be moving from the phone to the Net.

12. There will be speed bumps on the Internet.

In spite of our rosy predictions, the Internet faces two speed bumps in the near future.

One is the Internet bubble itself. Just because two guys under thirty start a Website with $30 million in venture-capital funds doesn't automatically make the site worth $3 billion. Sooner or later, reality will sink in.

In spite of the enormous acceptance, it's going to be difficult to make money on the Net. The Internet is a high-volume, low-margin medium. In other words, a price game. We don't believe that investors truly understand the nature of this medium—yet. While the Internet is wildly popular, it is not wildly profitable. And profit is what Wall Street ultimately seeks.

With combined sales of $24 billion (and combined losses of $7 billion), the 241 major Internet companies have a stock market value of $549 billion. Sooner or later, the bubble will burst.

If you own any Internet stocks, you should read *The Internet Bubble* by Anthony B. Perkins and Michael C. Perkins, editors at *Red Herring* magazine. The Perkins brothers are not rabble-rousers, but insiders who cover the venture-capital industry on a daily basis. Their prediction of a coming shakeout is frightening.

The Internet will survive and prosper. But many Internet companies will not.

The second speed bump along the way is the tax issue. Currently there is a three-year moratorium on state and federal taxes. (The Internet Tax Freedom Act was passed in 1998.)

That will change. The 46 states, 4,831 cities, and 1,151 counties that impose sales taxes are not going to give the Internet a free ride forever. Sooner or later they are going to want their cut.

The Apple iBook we recently purchased on the Net would have cost $111.72 more (to cover taxes) if bought locally. Sooner or later, the governor, the mayor, or the county tax commissioner is going to want to get their hands on that $111.72 You can count on it.

What's next? What will come after the Internet? What will be the technological revolution of the first decade of the next millennium? Who knows?

- It could be the optical computer with photons carrying the ball in place of electrons. Such a development could drastically reduce the size and increase the speed and memory capacities of all computing devices, making a mockery of Moore's law.

- It could be a new engine, light in weight, highly efficient, and ultrapowerful. Such a development could revolutionize the transportation industries: automotive, aircraft, shipping, railroad.

- It could be a new development in genetics, especially in the field of agriculture. Such a development could revolutionize the way crops are planted, grown, and harvested.

Whatever the future brings, you can be sure of one thing: It will be a destabilizing development. It will change the way you manage your business and the way you build your brands.

And there will be a new book:

The Immutable Laws of _____ Branding.

Maybe we will write it, maybe we won't. But you can be sure that somebody will.

Index

165

167

173